# THE NIGERIAN NATION AND RELIGION

# THE NIGERIAN NATION AND RELIGION

## (INTERFAITH SERIES, VOL. I)

Hyacinth Kalu

iUniverse, Inc.
Bloomington

# THE NIGERIAN NATION AND RELIGION (INTERFAITH SERIES, VOL. I)

*iUniverse books may be ordered through booksellers or by contacting:*

*iUniverse*
*1663 Liberty Drive*
*Bloomington, IN 47403*
*www.iuniverse.com*
*1-800-Authors (1-800-288-4677)*

*ISBN: 978-1-4620-2736-1 (pbk)*
*ISBN: 978-1-4620-2947-1 (ebk)*

*Library of Congress Control Number: 2011909311*

*Printed in the United States of America*

*iUniverse rev. date: 06/10/2011*

*To my friends, benefactors and parishioners
of St. Lorenzo Ruiz Catholic Community,
Walnut, California, United States of America,
in gratitude for their love and support.*

# ACKNOWLEDGEMENT

My greatest thanks and praise goes to God Almighty for the many graces and favors He has shown to me. I also give thanks and honor to the Blessed Virgin Mary for her maternal love and intercessions, and to my little angel Agnes Chikaodinaka Kalu.

My studies in the United States of America and the writing of this book would not have been successful without the help and support of some special people to whom I owe lots of gratitude and appreciation. Worth mentioning among these people are my parents Mr. Maurice Kalu Arunsi and Mrs. Felicia Ogonnaya Kalu, the International Buddhist Education Foundation, Mr. and Mrs. Sam and Sue Tolfa, Most Rev. Lucius Iwejuru Ugorji, Prof. Kenneth A. Locke, and friends and parishioners of St. Lorenzo Ruiz Catholic Church, Walnut California, USA. I equally extend my gratitude to my colleagues and Professors at the University of the West, Rosemead, California, USA.

To you my brothers and sisters, friends, and benefactors, I say thank you for your gifts of presence and love in my life.

# TABLE OF CONTENTS

# LIST OF ABBREVIATIONS

| | |
|---|---|
| AD | Anno Domini |
| AH | Anno Hegirae or After Hegira |
| ATR | African Traditional Religion |
| BCE | Before the Common Era |
| CAN | Christian Association of Nigeria |
| CCN | Christian Council of Nigeria |
| CE | Common Era |
| CKC | Christ the King Church |
| CMS | Church Missionary Society |
| COCIN | Church of Christ in Nigeria |
| CPFN | Christian Pentecostal Fellowship of Nigeria |
| CSN | Catholic Secretariat of Nigeria |
| CWO | Catholic Women's Organization |
| CWR | Council for World Religions |
| ECWA | Evangelical Church of West Africa |
| FESTAC | Festival of Arts and Culture |
| ING | Interim National Government |
| IRCSL | Interreligious Council of Sierra Leone |
| JNI | Jama'atu Nasril Islam |
| LGA | Local Government Area |
| ₦ Naira. | (Nigerian Currency) |
| NGO | Non-Governmental Organization |
| NIREC | Nigeria Inter-religious Council |
| NIYF | Nigerian Interfaith Youth Forum |
| NPN | National Party of Nigeria |
| NPO | Non Profit Organization |
| NSCIA | Nigeria Supreme Council for Islamic Affairs |
| NT | New Testament |
| NYSC | National Youth Service Corp. |
| OAIC | Organization of African Instituted Churches |
| OIC | Organization of Islamic Conference (or Countries) |
| OT | Old Testament |
| OTRA | Organization of Traditional Religions of Africa |

| | |
|---|---|
| pbuh | peace be upon him. |
| SABM | Southern American Baptist Mission |
| SAC | Société Africaine de Culture |
| St. | Saint |
| TEKAN | Taraya Ekkilisiya Krist A Nigeria |
| UK | United Kingdom |
| UPN | Unity Party of Nigeria |
| US | United States |
| USA | United States of America |
| Vatican II | Second Vatican Council |
| *VS* | VERSUS |
| WCC | World Council of Churches |

# INTRODUCTION

Chinua Achebe, a renowned Nigerian professor, writing in the early 1980's, identified the Nigerian problem as leadership. In his words:

> The trouble with Nigeria is simply and squarely a failure of leadership. There is nothing basically wrong with the Nigerian character. There is nothing wrong with the Nigerian land or climate or water or air or anything else. The Nigerian problem is the unwillingness or inability of its leaders to rise to the responsibility, to the challenge of personal example which are (*sic*) the hallmarks of true leadership.[1]

Achebe might have been right to identify leadership as the only or at least the major problem with the Nigerian society from independence to the 80's, but today the problem is no longer leadership alone. The major problem that threatens the stability of Nigeria as one sovereign nation is religious. There are three dominant religions in Nigeria – African Traditional Religion (ATR), Islam and Christianity.

Since independence in 1960, religion has been a major factor in shaping the political landscape of Nigeria. Though a secular state[2]

---

[1]  Chinua Achebe, *The Problem with Nigeria*. (Enugu: Fourth Dimension Publishing Co. Ltd, 1983), 1.

[2]  The secularity of Nigerian State is that the federal, state and local governments or any other part of the government institution is not to adopt any religion as official. It not does remove the name of God or the use of such name in government establishments nor does do it stand against worship and prayer in such places

by definition, politicians use religion as a stepping-stone to power and political legitimacy. As observed by Falola:

> Since the mid-seventies, politicians have urged their followers to vote along religious lines – Muslims are told to vote for Muslims, and Christians for Christians. In 1978, the National Party of Nigeria (NPN) told it followers in one of its strong Islamic northern constituencies that the two-fingered V-for-victory sign of the Unity Party of Nigeria (UPN) was a covert symbol of polytheism, an idea counter to fundamental Islamic doctrine. The NPN adopted one raised finger as their symbol, turning the universal (and universally secular) V sign into a [politico] religious issue. Later, on the eve of the 1979 presidential elections, Sheikh Abubakar Gumi advised Nigerian Muslims, in a speech broadcast nationally, not to vote for a non-Muslim candidate. The 1990 gubernatorial elections in Lagos and Kaduna were deeply affected by religious issues, and the primary process for the 1993 election of a civilian president was complicated by conflicts between Muslim and Christian candidates.[3]

Election to the highest political office in Nigeria is determined by religious affiliation. The first question that comes out of people's lips is: is the candidate Christian or Muslim or a follower of ATR? Appointments to political offices are made in line with religious identifications. In some parts of the country, a person has to strongly manifest a tendency towards a particular religion before he/she is offered a job. Even the ethnic divisions and geopolitical zones in Nigeria are closely identified along the line of religious divide. This connection between religion and ethnicity in Nigerian is clearly evident in Paul Oranika's presentation of the ethnic make up of Nigeria:

---

[3] Toyin Falola, *Violence in Nigeria: The Crisis of Religious Politics and Secular Ideologies.* (New York: University of Rochester press, 1998), 2.

Nigeria, Africa's most populous nation, has over 250 ethnic groups. The most influential ethnic groups include the Hausa/Fulani in the north, who are mostly Muslims representing about 28% of the total population. The Yorubas and the Igbo are the most dominant ethnic groups in the south. They are mostly Christians, representing 21% and 19% of the total population respectively. Other ethnic groups include: Ijaw; mostly Christians, 9%, Kanuri; mostly Muslims, 4%, Ibibio; mostly Christians, 3.6%, and Tiv, 2.7 %. (*sic*)"[4]

This data confirms the fact that even ethnic rivalries, which are also a problem in today's Nigeria, have religious undertones in most cases.

However, there is one important question that needs to be asked: Is religion in itself an instrument of violence or peace? This question could be answered by looking at the essence or nature of religion itself, and by looking at the activities of the religious followers in the name of religion.

Essentially, religion is an instrument of peace rather than violence; it teaches people to make society a better place through its message of peace, unity, and love. There is no religion that preaches violence and conflict as basic doctrines of belief or as a way of life.

On the other hand, religious adherents often employ religion as instrument of violence and conflicts. In the words of Leo D. Lefebure,

> Religious traditions promise to heal the wounds of human existence by uniting humans to ultimate reality; yet the history of religion is steeped in blood, war, sacrifice, and scapegoating. While many interpreters of religion have focused on the constructive role of religion in human life, the brutal facts of history of religions impose the stark realization of the intertwining of religion and violence: violence, clothed in religious garb, has repeatedly cast a

---

[4]  Paul Oranika, *Nigeria: One Nation, Two Systems.* (Baltimore: PublishAmerica, 2004), 16.

spell over religion and culture, luring countless "decent" people – from unlettered peasants to learned priests, preachers, and professors – into its destructive dance.[5]

Religion, that supposedly "pure" thing, has unfortunate become a double-aged sword, bringing good and bad, joy and sorrow, peace and violence, depending on who is using it and for what purpose he or she is using it. Emphasizing this fact, James Wellman writes,

Religion kills. Religion brings peace . . . Religion, conflict, and violence have intersected throughout history and across religious traditions . . . Religion functions as an identity-forming mechanism that constructs and mobilizes individuals and groups, both to violence as well to peace. Religion, like politics, forms identities and thus the two cannot help but move in relation to one another, sometimes antagonistically and sometimes tandem. Politics, power, coercion, and religion may be strange bedfellows but they are structurally linked. Thus to say that religion is either always innocent or always evil is misguided.[6]

To restore religion to its rightful "glory" as an instrument of love and harmony and to build a consensus of co-existence and mutual understanding among people of various religious affiliations and communities is a crucial task for religious leaders and adherents. This crucial task can successfully be handled by understanding the purpose of religion, which is making humans better and cultivating spirituality; and by moving beyond what divides us so to what unites us. In this, we can cooperate with each other to make our nation, Nigeria, loving and peaceful.

---

5    Leo D. Lefebure, *Revelation, the Religions, and Violence*. (New York: Orbis Books, 2000), 13.

6    James K. Wellman, Jr., "Religion and Violence: Past, Present, and Future," in James K. Wellman's ed., *Belief and Bloodshed: Religion and Violence across Time and Tradition*. (New York: Rowman & Littlefield Publishers, Inc., 2007), 1.

This work, which is a-three-volume series on interfaith relationships in Nigeria, looks into the various ways that we can move beyond the religious differences between the three religions in Nigeria: African traditional religion, Islam, and Christianity, and live, work and co-exit peacefully with one another as sisters and brothers. Although volume one of this series begins with the history of Nigeria as nation, its primary concern, and indeed, the concern of the entire series, is not with the politics, economics, and culture of the Nigerian people *per se*, but with the religion of the people. Hence, it is a study of African Traditional Religion, Islam, and Christianity in Nigeria. The focus is not the theological and dogmatic principles and faith life of these religions, nor the individual and various sects within these religions; rather these religions are studied from the standpoint of interfaith encounter and relationships.

The use of the term African Traditional Religion is problematic since Africa is not a spot but "the second largest continent in the world and the home to nearly 3,000 ethnic and linguistic groups totaling over 700 million people."[7] This large continent is multi-cultural and multi-religious. The religious beliefs and customs vary from tribe to tribe. However, due to the lack of an acceptable alternative, I have decided to use the term African Traditional Religion, with the proviso that, in this work, it only refers to the native and indigenous religious practices of the Nigerian people, and not the entire continent of Africa.

The intention of this work is not to solve all the religious problems in Nigeria, but to significantly advance our knowledge in the field of Religious Studies in Nigeria, and in the area of interfaith relationships among the three religions in Nigeria, as a contribution to the peace process and stability of the nation.

Again, although references will be made to other zones in Nigeria, major attention will be focused on the Northern zone and the South-Eastern zone. These two zones are the major theatres of

---

7    Lewis M. Hopfe, & Mark R. Woodward, *Religions of the World.* 8th Ed. (New Jersey: Prentice Hall, 2001), 49.

religious violence in Nigeria. As soon as violence occurs in one of these zones, it spreads to other geopolitical zones.

Particularly, this first volume of the interfaith series provides the foundation for the two other volumes. It contextualizes the geographical entity called Nigeria, and identifies the religions that thrive within it. In Nigeria, we have major or dominant religions as well as other minor religious groups and fraternities. Some of these groups and fraternities do not identify themselves as religions in strict sense of the word. This work, in its three volumes, revolves around the major religions in Nigeria: African Traditional Religion, Islam, and Christianity. The reason for focusing on these three is obvious: Religious violence and peace building in Nigeria always occur along the lines of African Traditional Religion, Islam, and Christianity. As for the other religions, it takes a scholar of religion to see their relevance in the Nigerian society. Ordinary Nigerians either do not feel their impact or classify them as secret cult that should be avoided.

This volume is divided into five chapters. Chapter one defines the object of our study: Nigeria as a nation. Chapter two defines the subject of our study: the three religions – African Traditional Religion, Islam, and Christianity – in Nigeria. Chapters three to five are discussions on the origins and historical developments of the three religions – African Traditional Religion, Islam, and Christianity – in Nigeria and the South-East geopolitical zone, beginning with a general overview of religion in Nigeria.

To put things straight, what do we mean by the term origin in the study of religion, and what are we looking for to establish such origin? Responding to this question, Alfred Garvie pointed out that the term "origin with reference to religion is ambiguous and implies that it is necessary for the scholar to make clear in his own mind what he actually seeks to know as he approaches this baffling and elusively delicate subject."[8] Analyzing Garvie's statement on the origin of religion, Bolaji Idowu said:

---

[8]    Alfred E. Garvie, *The Christian Belief in God in Relation to Religion and Philosophy.* (London: Hodder and Stoughton, 1933), 88

According to Garvie, the word 'origin' may represent the question: (a) What is the source of, and the reason for man's being religious in nature? (b) What is the source of, and reason for, man's being religious in the conditions of the world in which he finds himself? (c) What is the earliest form in which religion has appeared, so far as we can trace back to its development?[9]

Applying the above analysis to our study of the origins of the three religions in Nigeria and the South-East, we are not just looking at the founders, or historical dates. We are also looking at the people among whom the religion originated, the environment that gave birth to the religion or made the implantation of such religion possible as well as factors that facilitated its development. We are looking at the religious experience and expression of the people among whom the religion is said to have originated.

Finally, this volume will end with a conclusion, which at the same time will prelude the second volume in this series of interfaith relationships in Nigeria.

---

[9]  E. Bolaji Idowu, *African Traditional Religion: A Definition*. (New York: Orbis Books, 1975), 33.

# CHAPTER ONE

# NIGERIA AS A NATION

This chapter describes the political, social and cultural history of Nigeria as a nation from the beginnings of human habitation in the region up to this 21st century. The goal of this history is to provide us with the geographical location and outlook of life before the advent of Christianity and Islam in Nigeria, as well as the political landscape of today's Nigeria. There were no vacuum when the foreign and or missionary religions (Christianity and Islam) came to Nigeria; there were structures on the ground that made it possible for them to enter, establish themselves and spread. These structures are the political, social and cultural life of the people.

## 1.1 Nigeria as a Nation.

Most historians are accustomed to beginning the history of Nigeria from the independence and post-independence periods of the 1960s. But the basic truth is that the history of what today is called Nigeria dates to Before the Common Era (BCE)

Recent archaeological research has shown that people were already living in southwestern Nigeria (specifically Iwo-Eleru) as early as 9000 BCE and perhaps earlier at Ugwuelle-Uturu (Okigwe) in southeastern Nigeria (the history of South-Eastern Nigeria will be treated in a separate sub-heading). Archeological evidences show the existence of metalwork as early as the 4th century BCE in Taruga in the North. Microlithic and ceramic industries were also developed by savanna pastoralists at this period and were continued by subsequent agricultural communities. In the south, hunting and gathering gave way to subsistence farming in the first century BCE and the cultivation of staple foods.[10] The earliest documented Nigerian culture is that of the Nok people who thrived between 600 BCE and 200 CE on the Jos Plateau in northeastern Nigeria. Reporting on this, Falola writes, "There is evidence of iron technology used by the Nok people near the present-day Abuja."[11]

Information is lacking from the first millennium CE following the Nok ascendancy, but by the beginning of 2nd millennium CE (1000-1300 CE) much of the societies that make up modern Nigeria "developed loosely constructed decentralized state systems, while others developed into the first large scale centralized states of the region."[12] These early states included the Yoruba kingdoms, the Igbo kingdom of Nri, the Edo kingdom of Benin, Oyo and Ife kingdoms, the Efik kingdom, the Ibibio kingdom, the Annang kingdom, the Hausa cities, and Nupe. Numerous small states to the west and south of Lake Chad were absorbed or displaced in the course of the expansion of the Kanem-Borno Empire, which was centered to the northeast of Lake Chad.

Between 1300 and 1450 CE, there was active trade from North Africa through the Savanna (which occupies the east of the central area of Africa) to the forest of West Africa, the people of the Savanna acting as intermediaries in the exchange of goods. Toyin Falola and Matthew Heaton described this period as the "golden age of the trans-Saharan trade."[13]

The period 1450-1850 saw the first contact of Nigeria with Europe. Describing the events of this period, Toyin and Heaton write:

---

[10]   Toyin Falola & Matthew Heaton, *A History of Nigeria*. ( New York: Cambridge University Press, 2007 xiii.

[11]   Ibid.

[12]   Ibid, 21.

[13]   Falola & Heaton, *A History of Nigeria*, xiii

Contacts with Europeans on the coast from 1450-1850 resulted in monumental changes in the political, economic, and social institutions of southern Nigerian states. The trade in slaves dominated relations between Nigerians and Europeans at this time.[14]

The abolition of the slave trade and the expansion of British influence on trade with the West African interior saw the establishment of the Royal Niger Company in 1886, chartered under the leadership of Sir George Taubman Goldie. It was at this period that the British established a dominant influence on the region that is now called Nigeria. According to Paul Oranika,

> By 1885, the British consul office had signed treaties with the Fulani kingdom of Sokoto. Britain formed the Oil River Protectorate, including the Niger Delta and Calabar, following the end of the Berlin Conference. Subsequently, the territory was expanded in 1894 to include the Lagos colony and northwards mostly along the Niger River as far as the Lokoja town on the confluence of the river Niger and Benue. In 1897, Benin, Oyo, and Ijebu were brought into the Protectorate by treatise following the massacre of the British consul and his entourage, who were heading to Benin to investigate reports of human sacrifice in the old city.[15]

In 1900, the Royal Niger Company's territory came under the control of the British Government, which moved to consolidate its hold over the area of modern Nigeria. On January 1, 1901, Nigeria became a British protectorate, part of the British Empire, the foremost world power at the time, with Frederick Lugard as British Colonial Administrator.

---

[14]  Ibid.

[15]  Paul Oranika, Nigeria: *One Nation, Two Systems*. (Baltimore: PublishAmerica, 2004), 19.

In 1914, Frederick Lugard, who became the Governor-General, amalgamated the Northern and the Niger Coast protectorates as the Colony and Protectorate of Nigeria. This amalgamation is the birth of the Country. As reported by Simeon Ilensami, "Nigeria as a nation is a child of British colonialism. Its modern history appropriately begins on 1 January 1914, when two disparate territories –the northern and southern protectorates – were amalgamated under the administrative leadership of Lord Lugard."[16] Lugard administered this unified colonial state through a system dubbed 'indirect rule' that allowed, "The indigenous political institutions through the chiefs and elites to maintain local authority while submitting themselves to the authority of the central apparatus of British colonial administrators."[17]

Nigeria was granted full independence in October 1, 1960 under a constitution that provided for a parliamentary government and a substantial measure of self-government. From 1959 to 1960, Jaja Wachuku was the First black Speaker of the Nigerian Parliament—also called the House of Representatives. Wachuku replaced Sir Frederick Metcalfe of Great Britain. Notably, as First Speaker of the House, Jaja Wachuku received Nigeria's Instrument of Independence—also known as Freedom Charter—on October 1, 1960, from Princess Alexandra of Kent, the Queen's representative at the Nigerian independence ceremonies. The nationalist movements that gave birth to the Independence of Nigeria was led by leaders such as Nnamdi Azikiwe, Obafemi Awolowo, and Sir Abubakar Tafawa Balewa

In October 1963 Nigeria proclaimed itself a Federal Republic and former Governor General Nnamdi Azikiwe became the country's first President, with Abubakar Tafawa Balewa as the first Prime Minister.

On January 15, 1966 a group of army officers, mostly southeastern Igbos, who felt that the Igbos were marginalized

---

[16]    Simeon O. Ilesanmi, Religious Pluralism and the Nigerian State. ((Ohio: Center for International Studies, 1997), 121-122.

[17]    Falola & Heaton, *A History of Nigeria*, 6.

and not given their share in the power-sharing and economy of the country, overthrew the federal government and assassinated the prime minister and the premiers of the northern and western regions. This coup saw the first military regime in Nigeria, with General Johnson Thomas Umunnakwe Aguiyi Ironsi, as Head of State. This coup will later be seen as a coup against the Muslims, and incidentally led to the Nigeria-Biafra civil war of 1967-1970 that was not only seen as an ethnic war, but a religious war between the Muslim North and the Christian South.

This first incursion of the military into politics that terminated Nigeria's first republic lasted until 1979 when democratic governance returned to Nigeria, this time with a constitution that provided for a presidential system of government, thus ushering in the second republic with Alhaji Shehu Shagari as the First Executive President of Nigeria.

The second republic came to its sudden death on December 31, 1983 with a military coup that saw Major General Muhammadu Buhari as the Head of State. General Ibrahim Babangida removed Buhari from office through a coup in 1985. Again, this period lasted until 1993, which saw the abortive third republic planned and cancelled by General Babangida, then President and Head of State, with the annulment of the June 12, 1993 Presidential election acclaimed to have been won by M.K.O Abiola. A majority of Nigerians saw the annulment of the June 12 election as having a religious undertone. The Muslim North in their quest to dominate the political scene of Nigeria could not bear the sight of a Southerner as president, as that would undermine their plan of registering Nigeria into to Organization of Islamic Countries (OIC), which was a very hot topic at the time.

The annulment of the election and the stepping aside of General Babangida brought in Chief Ernest Shonekan, who was appointed the head of the Interim National Government (ING) in August 26, 1993. The Minister of Defense General Sani Abacha removed him from office through a staged coup on November 17, 1993. General Sani Abacha, Head of State, President and commander-in-Chief of the armed forces, relinquished power only at his death in 1998.

His death brought in General Abdusalami Abubakar to power. This period of military dictatorship came to an end in 1999 when power was handed over to a democratically elected president, Olusegun Obasanjo, former Military Head of State in 1976-1979, on May 29, 1999; thus ending a 16 year military rule. This transition saw the emergence of the present 4th republic that has witnessed a smooth transition of power from one democratic government to another, with Umaru Yar'adua elected as president in 2007. Yar'dua died in office on May 5, 2010 giving way to the Vice President Goodluck Ebere Jonathan being sworn in as current President on May 6, 2010. Of the fifty years of Nigeria Independence, the military has ruled twenty-eight years.

Present day Nigeria is the most populous nation in Africa, and the largest country in the West African region,[18] with a population of 140,003,542 according to the most recent census of March 21-28, 2006.[19] The population was estimated at about 150,000,000 in 2009, given the "population growth estimated at 2.38% each year."[20] The country measures about 923,768 square kilometers, making it slightly more than twice the size of California.[21] It is bordered to the south by the Bights of Benin and Biafra, which are on the gulf of Guinea in the Atlantic Ocean. On the west Nigeria is bordered by Benin, on the north by Niger, and on the east by Cameroon. In its extreme northeastern corner, Lake Chad separates Nigeria from the country of Chad. The country stretches "roughly 700 miles from west to east and 650 miles from south to north, covering an area between 3° and 15°E longitude and between 4° and 14° latitude."[22]

---

[18] Toyin Falola and Matthew M. Heaton, *A History of Nigeria* (Cambridge: Cambridge University Press, 2008), 2.

[19] John N. Paden, *Faith and Politics in Nigeria.* (Washington, D.C.: U.S. Institute of Peace Press, 2008), 5.

[20] Ibid.

[21] *Nigeria: Central Intelligence Agency. The World FactBook.* https:// www.cia.gov/library/publications/the-world-factbook/geos/ ni.html (accessed: March 11,2009)

[22] Falola & Heaton, *A History of Nigeria*, 2.

The estimated number of Ethno-linguistic groups in Nigeria range between 250 and 400, depending on how dialects and subgroups are counted. Nevertheless, three major ethnic groups dominate in Nigeria, namely, "Hausa/Fulani (29 percent) in the north; Yoruba (21 percent) in the southwest; and Igbo (18 percent) in the southeast. Thus, these three tribal groups constitute about 68 percent of the national population. In addition, there are a number of midsize ethnolinguistic groups."[23] Among the additional hundreds of minorities ethnic groups are:

> Ijaw (10 percent) in the south-south; Kanuri (4 percent) in the Middle Belt; Ibibio (3.5 percent) also in the south-south; and Tiv (2.5 percent) in the Middle Belt. There are dozens of smaller groups especially in the Middle Belt and south-south areas.[24]

The ethnolinguistic differences not withstanding, English is the official language, Hausa, Yoruba, and Igbo are designated as national languages because they are the major ethnic groups in Nigeria, and are found in parts of the country in large numbers.

The government bureaucracy has three tiers – federal, state, and local – with each guaranteed certain responsibilities by the Nigerian Constitution. The country is divided into thirty-six states, a Federal Capital Territory, and 774 local government areas. The states are grouped into six geopolitical zones, with the South-East being one of them.

Economically, Nigeria is a rich agricultural country, producing large quantities of cocoa, peanuts, palm oil, corn, rice, sorghum, millet, cassava (tapioca), yams, rubber, cotton, cattle, sheep, goats, pigs, timber, and fish.[25] The country is richly blessed with abundant mineral resources that include crude oil, coal, tin, columbite and

---

[23]   Paden, *Faith and Politics in Nigeria*, 7.

[24]   Ibid.

[25]   *Nigeria: Central Intelligence Agency. The World FactBook.* https://www.cia.gov/library/publications/the-world-factbook/geos/ni.html (accessed: March 19,2009)

cement.[26] However, the economy of Nigeria is mostly dependent on oil. The country is "the leading oil exporter in Africa and world's eighth largest oil producing nation."[27]

Culturally, Nigerians are influenced both by their indigenous traditions and by westernization. Traditional reliance on extended family and kinship networks remains strong throughout Nigeria, but a growing reliance on smaller nuclear families and on individual achievement is also being recognized. While polygamy is a common practice in the country, monogamous marriage is also common, particularly among Christians and the educated elites.

Having discussed the geographical entity and location we are dealing with in this work: Nigeria as nation and the South East as one of the geopolitical zones in Nigeria, we shall now proceed to discuss the origin and historical developments of the three religions in Nigeria, namely, African Traditional Religion, Islam and Christianity.

---

[26]    Ibid.

[27]    Falola & Heaton, *A History of Nigeria*, 11

# CHAPTER TWO

## RELIGION IN NIGERIA: AN OVERVIEW.

Nigerians are deeply religious, to the point that "loyalty to religion is often more important than loyalty to the state."[28] There are three dominant religions in Nigeria: African Traditional Religion, Islam, and Christianity.[29] The oldest of these religions is African Traditional Religion (ATR), which is the indigenous religion of the people. Islam entered Nigeria in the 11th century, with Christianity making its first attempt in the 15th century and finally succeeding in the 19th century.[30] In Nigeria, African Traditional Religion, which "consists of a variety of localized religious practices and beliefs",[31] is united under the umbrella of the Organization of Traditional Religions of Africa (OTRA).[32] The Muslims are united under the umbrella of

---

[28]    Toyin, *Violence in Nigeria*, 50.

[29]    Cyril O. Imo, *Religion and the Unity of the Nigerian Nation.* (Uppsala: Almqvist & Wiksell International, 1995), 7.

[30]    Ibid, 17-18

[31]    Ibid, 17.

[32]    The Organization of Traditional Religions of Africa was formed by K.O.K. Onyioha Eze Ewelu Ochie II, the king of Ukwa Ukwu, Nkporo, Nigeria in the mid-1970s, in conjunction with a group of well educated Igbos, and Oba Akenzua II, the king of Benin. These people sought to rekindle interest in the traditional African forms of religion, rather than the foreign religions of Christianity and Islam.

the Supreme Council of Islamic Affairs (SCIA), and the Christians under the umbrella of the Christian Association of Nigeria (CAN).

Besides the three dominant religions mentioned above, there are other religious bodies and fraternities that manifest one or more characteristic of religion in Nigeria. Among these are Judaism, Hinduism-Hare Krishna Society, Baha'i, Satguru Maharaj Ji Movement, Rosicrucian Order, Grail Message, Reformed Ogboni Fraternity, Freemasonry, and Eckankar.

## 2.1 The Three Major Religions in Nigeria: African Traditional Religion, Islam, and Christianity.

When mention is made of religion in Nigeria, what comes to mind are the three major and dominant religions, namely, African Traditional Religion, Islam, and Christianity.

Affiliation to these religions in Nigeria is strongly related to ethnicity, colored with tribal and regional sentiments. The northern states, dominated by the Hausa and Fulani groups, are predominantly Muslim while the southeastern ethnic group has a large number of Christians. In the southwest, there is no predominant religion. The Yoruba tribe, which is the majority ethnic group in the southwest, practices Christianity, Islam, and/or the traditional Yoruba religion, which centers on the belief in one supreme god and several lesser deities. Traditional religionists have no territory as such in Nigeria, they are scattered all over. Affirming the ethnic undertone of religious divide in Nigeria, Ilesanmi writes, "Studies have shown that the historic formation of most Nigeria's ethnic groups not only had specific religious roots, but also that their continuing self-fashioning and self-definition are heavily influenced by their religious assumptions."[33]

Overall statistics of religion in Nigeria indicate that about 50% of the populations are Muslim, with a majority practicing the Sunni branch of the faith. About 40% are Christian and about

---

[33]  Ilesanmi, *Religious Plurality and the Nigerian State*, 115.

10% practice traditional African religions.[34] This analysis shows a drastic decline of African traditional religion from what it used to be in 1900. A survey conducted by Barrett in 1982 represented and projected the religious percentage of the three religions in Nigeria between 1900 and 2000 as follow:[35]

| RELIGION | 1900 | 1970 | 1980 | 2000 |
|----------|------|------|------|------|
| A T R | 73.0 | 10.8 | 5.6 | 3.0 |
| CHRISTIANITY | 1.1 | 44.9 | 49.0 | 51.2 |
| ISLAM | 25.3 | 44.0 | 45.0 | 45.4 |

Although the percentage of those who profess Islam and Christianity have increased considerably within the last 100 years, while those who profess traditional religion has decreased, many people in Nigeria today include elements of traditional beliefs in their own practice of Christianity or Islam. While professing officially Christians and Muslim, they resort to Indigenous religious practices and beliefs in their day-to-day life. It is on record that:

> Across Nigeria, churches or mosques can be found in virtually every settlement: evidence of deep Christian and Muslim roots sown by the merchants, missionaries and slave traders who brought the religions hundreds of years ago. But also firmly settled in the red soil are indigenous religious practices that Nigerians integrate with the foreign beliefs.[36]

---

[34]  Paden, *Faith and Politics in Nigeria*, 7.
[35]  David Barrett, *World Christian Encyclopedia*. (Nairobi: Oxford Press, 1982), 527.
[36]  "Nigerians meld Christianity, Islam with ancient practices" in *World Wide Religious News*. ( October 14, 2007) accessed: March 22,

Let us cite few examples of this mixture of Christianity and Islam with Traditional religion to prove our point that although African Traditional Religion is given a small percentage compared to Christian and Islam in Nigeria, a number of Christians and Muslims can be describe as ***Christraditionalists*** and ***Muslitraditionalists***[37] respectively, for lack of better words. To begin with the Christians, using the words of Idowu:

> It is now becoming clear to the most optimistic of Christian evangelists that the main problem of the church in Africa today is the divided loyalties of most of her members between Christianity with its Western categories and practices on one hand, and the traditional religion on the other.[38]

The words of a Zairean poet further express the situation, "Oh unhappy Christian, Mass in the morning, witch doctor in the evening. Amulet (Charm) in the pocket, Bible in the hand and scapular/medals around the neck."[39]

> Among the Muslims, the situation is the same. For example:
>
> In Oshogbo, Nigeria—Wasiu Olasunkani drops to his knees in the sacred grove, lowers his chin to his chest and turns his palms skyward: a gesture of thanks to a traditional water goddess embodied by the massive stone

---

2009. http://www.wwrn.org/article.php?idd=26568&sec=con=60

[37] Christraditionalists and Muslitraditionalist are terms that I personally coined to describe Christians and Muslims who combine their Christianity and Islam with African Traditional Religion. These terms refer to those who are half-half: Half Christian-Half Traditionalist, and Half Muslim-Half Traditionalist.

[38] E. Bolaji Idowu, *African Traditional Religion: A Definition.* (New York: Orbis Books, 1975), 205-6.

[39] Nathaniel I. Ndiokwere, *The African Church, Today and Tomorrow, vol. I.* (Onitsha: Effective Key Publisher, 1994), 53.

idol with outstretched arms that sweep over an ancient shrine. Olasunkani, a Muslim whose 1998 pilgrimage to Mecca fulfilled one of the five pillars of Islam, joins tens of thousands of ethnic Yoruba people each year to pray before the idol and offer libations to her mermaid-like spirit, Osun. Last year, Olasunkani beseeched the goddess for a baby. This year he's thanking her for twin boys, Farook and Cordroy.[40]

The reason for the above situation is easily explained. Nigerians, like every other African tribe, look to religion for succor in strictly personal matters relating to the passages of life and the crises of life, like sickness, failure in business, death, witchcraft, and childlessness. This succor is not always found in the foreign religions of Islam and Christianity, hence the desire to get from their native religion what these other religions do not provide them with. In fact a number of Indigenous Christian Churches in Nigeria are African Traditional Religion oriented in their theology and rituals. Attesting to this fact from a personal Igbo experience, Cardinal Francis Arinze in a letter from the Pontifical Council for Interreligious Dialogue, Vatican City, addressed to the Presidents of the Episcopal Conferences of Africa and Madagascar, dated March 25, 1988 said:

> Many Christians, at critical moments in their lives, have recourses to practices of the traditional religion, or to 'prayer houses', 'healing homes', 'prophets', witchcraft or fortune-tellers. Some tend to join sects or so-called "Independent Churches" where they feel that certain elements of their culture are more respected.[41]

Expressing this view further, Ndiokwere said:

---

[40]  "Nigerians meld Christianity, Islam with ancient practices" accessed: March 22, 2009.

[41]  Francis Arinze, *Pastoral Attention to African Traditional Religion.* http://www.afrikaworld.net/afrel/vatican.html (accessed May 22, 2008)

> Because the European brand of Christianity was neither satisfying to the African, nor did it provide answers or solution to certain African problems . . . there has for long therefore been a painful search for something more satisfying and meaningful to the Africans, especially in the religious sphere . . . He looks for protective charms and amulets and other substances from anywhere."[42]

This anywhere is, of course, outside Christianity and Islam. A mixture of traditional rituals and sacrifices and prayers with the Christian and Muslim rites and rituals often satisfies such longings. Religion is practically indistinguishable from most aspects of Nigerian life, both socially and politically.

## 2.2 Religious Politics in Nigeria.

Constitutionally, Nigeria is secular state. The 1999 Constitution of the Federal Republic of Nigeria has stipulations guiding the existence and practice of religion in Nigeria. Article 10 of the constitution clearly states:

The Government of the Federation or of a State shall not adopt any religion as State Religion.[43]

On the practice of religion and worship in Nigeria, the Constitution states:

> i) Every person shall be entitled to freedom of thought, conscience and religion, including freedom to change his religion or belief, and freedom (either alone or in community with others, and in public or in private) to manifest and propagate his religion or belief in worship, teaching, practice and observance. ii) No person attending any place of education shall be required to

---

[42] Ndiokwere, *The African Church, Today and Tomorrow*, vol. I, 36-7.

[43] Article 10, 1999 Constitution of the Federal Republic of Nigeria.

> receive religious instruction or to take part in or attend
> any religious ceremony or observance if such instruction,
> ceremony or observance relates to a religion other than his
> own, or religion not approved by his parent or guardian.
> iii) No religious community or denomination shall
> be prevented from providing religious instruction for
> pupils of that community or denomination in any place
> of education maintained wholly by that community or
> denomination.[44]

Although the constitution prohibits state and local governments from declaring an official religion, a number of states have recently adopted various forms of the Islamic criminal and civil law known as Shari'ah, a move that many Christians believe to be an adoption of Islam as the de facto religion. The constitution also provides for freedom of religion. However, some states have restricted religious demonstrations, processions, or gatherings as a matter of public security. Business owners and public officials have been known to discriminate against individuals of a faith different from their own in matters of providing services and hiring practices.

Politically, Nigeria, as secular state should not mix politics with religion and vice versa, but the day-to-day practice of religion and governance in Nigeria shows that there exists a strong marriage between religion and politics in Nigeria. Largely religion has a dominant influence in Nigeria political life. This 'marriage' is traceable back to pre-colonial Nigeria. In pre-colonial Nigeria, different kingdoms, based on indigenous beliefs, often fused the roles of religious and temporal leader together. Thus, traditional politics of the people had a strong linkage to the belief in theocracy. For example, among the Yorubas, the *Oba* (king), who is the political leader of the people, only holds office in trust for *Olodumare* (the Supreme Being). Moreover, before an *Oba* is selected or appointed, as the case may be, the *Ifa* oracle must be adequately consulted for

---

[44]   Article 38 (section i-iii), 1999 Constitution of the Federal Republic
of Nigeria.

spiritual approval. Politics and religion in traditional society were intertwined; they influenced and enriched each other. Attesting this, Idowu writes:

> The pre-colonial Nigeria was monolithic, in that the sacred and the secular were not artificially bifurcated. Every adventure in life, as well as all instruments of governance and survival, were *(sic)* clothed in religious ritual, language, and symbolism.[45]

In the present-day Nigeria, the relationship has grown so deep as to raise some concerns. Commenting on this, Afe Adogame said:

> Religion has assumed an enigmatic stance in Nigeria in a fashion that [national] politics is almost being supplanted by religious politics. Islam perceives state power as quintessential in the advance and propagation of religion. The perceived Muslim domination of power and the inequitable distribution of national resources have led to a Christian scramble for a role in national public life . . . It is glaring that the interplay of religion and politics is intricately linked with the virulent competition for national resources.[46]

The political crisis of Nigeria's First Republic under Nnamdi Azikiwe and Tafawa Balewa is attributed to religious factor. As soon as Nigeria achieved political independence in 1960, the premier of the Northern region, Sir Ahmadu Bello, who was the Sarduna of Sokoto, embarked on a religious expansionism that became the cornerstone of religious politics in the nascent nation. Southerners accused the ruling Northern elite of indirectly pushing Islam to

---

[45]  Idowu, *African Traditional Religion: A Definition*, 84.

[46]  Afe Adogame, "Politicization of Religion and Religionization of Politics in Nigeria", in *Religion, History, and Politics in Nigeria: Essays in Honor of Ogbu U. Kalu.* Edited by Chima J. Korieh & Ugo G. Nwokeji. (New York: University of America Press, 2005), 130.

enlarge the Sokoto Caliphate. Ahmadu Bello, for example, was actively engaged with traditional rulers from the Middle Belt region where religion was openly traded for political positions.[47] The counter effect of this situation was the first military coup in Nigeria led by the Christian officer, Chukwuma Nzeogwu in 1966, and the subsequent Nigeria-Biafra civil war of 1967-1970.[48] Religious politics reached its height in Nigeria with the registration of Nigeria as a permanent member of the Organization of Islamic Countries during the administration of Ibrahim Babangida in 1986. In 2000, Ahmed Sani, governor of Zamfara state in the northwest, oversaw the implementation of a new law that extended Sharia to criminal matters in the State. Federal and State government continue to spend money in the building of religious places and funding of activities like pilgrimages to Mecca and Jerusalem. In almost all the government houses there are either a Mosque or a Chapel. Politicians in Nigeria openly employ religion as an instrument for securing votes and winning elections. A political analyst observed that:

> Religious sentiments have dominated political campaigns
> for general election . . . such development portended
> grave dangers for the nation's democracy . . . politicians
> use religion to misinform the people, they use religion to
> neutralize resistance, they use religion to justify injustice
> in the society and they use religion to bring division
> among the people.[49]

Apart from having overbearing influence on the political life of the nation, religion has also been a source of tension in Nigeria. Observing the scenario, Adogame said:

> Religion assumes political significance and generates
> tension due to the country's plurality. The tension has
> a clear connection with the growth of uncompromising
> Muslim and Christian activism, which has led to a

---

[47]   Ibid, 126.
[48]   Ibid, 126-127.
[49]   Ibid, 135.

growing culture of religious violence, particularly in the north. While three religions are involved, issues and conflicts have revolved largely around Islam and Christianity.[50]

The quest for converts and subsequent expansion by Christianity and Islam has created various forms of internal problems for some communities in Nigerian where relationships had been largely non-confrontational. Most students of political science are agreed on the fact that religion is one of the most dangerous threats to the attainment of full democratic process and stability in Nigeria.[51]

The involvement of religion in politics and its role in violence, not withstanding, religion has also been source of peace and development in the country. Religion has done more good than harm. In pre-colonial Nigeria and traditional societies, religion was the only source of harmony, peace, and order in the society. Presently, religion has continued to nurture the spirituality and life of the nation. It has been the conscience of the nation. Articulating some of the contributions of religion in the national and individual life of Nigerians, Awolalu writes:

> In addition to western education, medicine and technology also came through the missionaries. These improved people's health, reduced infant mortality, put under control diseases and ailments, which people dreaded and discouraged superstition and fear and brought better conditions of living.[52]

---

[50]   Ibid, 126

[51]   Matthew Hassan Kukah, *Democracy and Civil Society in Nigeria.* (Ibadan: Spectrum Books, 2003), 93.

[52]   Joseph Omosade Awolalu, "The Encounter Between Traditional and Other Religions", *in African Traditional Religions in Contemporary Society,* edited by Jacob Olupona. (New York: Paragon House, 1991), 114.

# CHAPTER THREE

# THE ORIGIN AND HISTORY OF AFRICAN TRADITIONAL RELIGION IN NIGERIA AND THE SOUTH-EAST ZONE.

African Traditional Religion is the primal religion of the people of Nigeria and the South-East zone. It has no specific beginning in terms of date, and "it has no founder."[53] It is a religion that grew out of human experience and expression beginning with the first appearance of human life in Nigeria, which, is traceable back to "as early as 9000 BC."[54] Describing the origin of African Traditional Religion, John Mbiti stated that:

> African traditional religion evolved slowly through many centuries, as people responded to the situations of their life and reflected upon their experiences. Many factors played a part in its development. These include the geographical environment – mountains, rivers, deserts and forests – the change of the seasons, the powers of nature (such as earthquakes, thunderstorms

---

[53]   John S. Mbiti, *African Religions and Philosophy*, 2nd ed. (London: Heinemann, 1989), 4

[54]   Toyin Falola & Matthew Heaton, *A History of Nigeria*. (New York: Cambridge University Press, 2007 xiii.

and volcanoes), calamities, epidemics, diseases, birth and death, major historical events like wars, locust invasion, famines, migrations and so on. To these must be added man's reflection on the universe, the question about its origin, the earth, the sky, the problem of evil and suffering, the phenomena of nature, and many other problems. Religious ideas and practices among the natives arose and took shape in the process of a man's search for answers to these questions, and as a way to make life safer and better.[55]

The religious practices in Nigeria and the Southeast that is collectively called African Traditional Religion are not the product or initiative of any single individual. Thus, African Traditional Religion is a product of the thinking and experience of the (Nigerian/ Igbo) forefathers and mothers, that is, men and women of former generations. They formed "religious ideas, formulated religious beliefs, they observed religious rituals and ceremonies, and they told proverbs and myths that carried religious meaning."[56] These were transmitted from one generation to another. Although the ATR is "the indigenous belief of the forefathers which emerged from the sustaining faith held by the forbearers of the present generation,"[57] without a founder or reformer, it nevertheless "incorporate heroes, leaders, priests, and priestess and other famous men and women in the body if its mythology."[58] The religion is not a missionary religion. This may have accounted for its gradual fading away among many communities in Nigeria and Igbo land. Again, it has no scripture

---

[55] John S. Mbiti, *Introduction to African Religion*, 2nd ed. (Ibadan: Heinemann, 1991), 16.

[56] Ibid, 13-14.

[57] Joseph Omosade Awolanu, "The Encounter between African Traditional Religion and Other Religions in Nigeria" in *African Traditional Religions in Contemporary Society*, edited by Jacob K. Olupona. (New York: Paragon House, 1991), 111.

[58] Mbiti, *African Religions and Philosophy*, 4.

like its counterparts in Nigeria—Islam and Christianity. As noted by Mbiti, "it is written in the history, the hearts and experiences of the people."[59]

Not being a missionary religion or having a scripture or holy book is both a plus and minus in the historical development of ATR. Commenting on this, Mbiti said,

> Having no sacred scriptures, it [ATR] has been able to move with the times, and it has produced no religious controversies. Different communities and people are free to hold different views and beliefs without the danger of being accused of heresy or falsehood. On the other hand, since there are no sacred books, we cannot tell precisely what African religion may have been five hundred years ago and how far it may have differed today from what it was many centuries ago. Therefore, we cannot speak of the purity of African religion, since there is no authority about what it was originally or at any given point in its history.[60]

ATR is an indispensible part of the people's cultural heritage. Because it developed together with all other aspects of the people's heritage, it belongs to the people within which it has evolved. Hence, we find differences in the ways in which the religious practices and ideas are ritualized from one Nigerian community to another. Where religious ideas and practices are borrowed or interchanged by neighboring communities, each people adapt them to suit their own requirement. It would be meaningless to try to transplant a whole set of native religious belief from one community to another local community, unless the people involved take it with themselves to such local community through a process of migration.

Again, although it adheres to the tradition of the people, ATR is not static. In its long history, it has undergone many changes from place to place and from time to time. Old ideas are dropped

---

[59]    Mbiti, *Introduction to African Religion*, 17
[60]    Ibid, 17.

when they are found to be irrelevant. For example, human sacrifice to the gods that was very much practiced in the past is no longer practiced today. African Traditional Religion is open to new ideas, and even new religions, and hence has been rightly described as the "first religious structure and substratum upon which Christianity and Islamic beliefs are overlaid."[61] Before the advent of Islam and Christianity, it was the only religion known to the Igbo people, to Nigerians and in the entire continent of Africa. As expressed by Anthony Njoku,

> Prior to the introduction of Islam, traditional religions were dominant in the north (of Nigeria). Fulani Jihad did not even completely root out these religions, but it progressively weakened their influence. In the south, which the influence of Islam did not penetrate as much as the north, traditional religions retained their influences, but the arrival of Christian missionaries and their employment of extra-religious tools and techniques to win converts considerably changed the religious landscape of the south.[62]

A glimpse of the influence ATR had in the history of the people can be seen in the statistics of the percentage it had in the 1900s.[63]

---

[61]   Ian Ritchie, *African Theology and Social Change: An Anthropological Approach.* ( Toronto: Wycliffe College, 1999), 102.

[62]   Anthony Chukwudi Njoku, "Economy, Politics, and the Theological Enterprise in Nigeria," in *Religion, History, and Politics in Nigeria: Essays in Honor of Ogbu U. Kalu.* Chima J. Korieh & G. Ugo Nwokeji, (eds). (New York: University Press of America, 2005), 142.

[63]   David Barrett, *World Christian Encyclopedia.* (Nairobi: Oxford Press, 1982), 175-768.

| COUNTRY | PERCENTAGE |
|---------|------------|
| BENIN | 91.8 |
| CAMEROUN | 96.4 |
| GABON | 92.5 |
| GHANA | 90.3 |
| COTE D'IVOIRE | 94.9 |
| KENYA | 95.8 |
| NIGERIA | 73.0 |
| TOGO | 95.1 |
| ZAIRE (CONGO) | 98.1 |
| ZAMBIA | 99.7 |
| ZIMBABWE | 96.0 |

African Traditional Religion in Nigeria and the South-East has continued to evolve and exercise much influence among various communities and people today, even among Muslims and Christians. The African identity and worldview, especially family oriented system, communal solidarity, respect for life and elders, sacred space and time, and many more are shaped and guided by the African religio-cultural system. In some communities, it appears stronger, while in some it appears to grow weaker.

# CHAPTER FOUR

# THE ORIGIN AND HISTORY OF ISLAM IN NIGERIA AND THE SOUTH-EAST ZONE.

In order to situate Islam within its global, national and local origins, we shall divide this chapter into two main sub-sections, beginning with the origin and history of Islam in Nigeria as nation, followed by the South-East (Igbo land) zone in particular.

## 4.1 The origin and history of Islam in Nigeria.

To understand Islam: its origin and history in Nigeria, this section will begin with a quick look at the origin and history of Islam in general, beginning in Mecca. This will help us to trace the route through which the religion entered Sub-Saharan Africa in general and Nigeria in particular.

4.1.1 The origin of Islam: An overview.

The Arabic word Islam is derived from the Semitic root word: *s l m*.[64] As a term, Islam comes directly from the Arabic: *Salam*.

---

[64]  Fazlur Rahman, "Islam: An Overview" in *Encyclopedia of Religion.* Ed, Lindsay Jones, Vol. 7, 2nd ed. (Detroit: Macmillan Reference USA, 2005). 4560.

The Arabic: "Salam or *salaama* may be translated as peace, purity, surrender, submission (to God) and obedience. Thus, Islam (in the religious context) means submission to and obedience to God's will and God's law."[65] Followers of Islam are called Muslims. A Muslims is "one who submits or surrenders to the will of Allah."[66] Thus, "the first man, Adam, who was also the first prophet, was a *Muslim* in the sense of being surrendered to God."[67] By extension, therefore, all who surrender to God, their religion not withstanding, including all the prophets before Muhammad including Jesus, are Muslims.

In terms of its origin, Muslims believe that Islam is not a new religion, but the original religion and same truth that God revealed to His prophets from the beginning of creation. Expressing and affirming this belief, Suzanne Haneef writes:

> Islam, meaning 'surrender' or 'submission', is the original religion revealed by God from the foundation of human history. He revealed it through the first man, Adam, who was also the first prophet. Later, revealed it to Abraham, the father of Judaism, Christianity and Islam . . . Still later, He revealed it through Moses, and afterwards, through Jesus Christ . . . and He revealed it for the last and final time through the prophet who established Islam as a world religion, Muhammad of Arabia, the most perfect of all mankind.[68]

---

[65]  Mark Water, *Encyclopedia of World Religions, Cults and the Occult.* (London: John Hunt Publishing Ltd, 2006), 99.

[66]  *Understanding Islam and the Muslims.* Prepared by The Islamic Affairs Department of The Embassy of Saudi Arabia, Washington DC, 1989, p.1

[67]  Suzanne Haneef, *Islam: The Path of God.* (Chicago: Kazi Publications, Inc., 1996), 7.
Rahman, Islam: An Overview, 4561

[68]  Haneef, *Islam: The Path of God,* 10.

Here, Islam is understood as "God's eternal religion, described in the Quran as 'the primordial nature upon which God created mankind' (30:30)."[69]

As a historical phenomenon, the origin of Islam is traced back to "the Hejaz, the western sector of Arabia from below the latitude of the Sinai Peninsula; a region where Islam was born and developed, and is thus called the 'cradle of Islam.'"[70] The Hejaz includes the present day cities of Mecca and Medina in Saudi Arabia. The historical data of the world's 2nd largest religion began properly with the life and message of a humble and uneducated, but trusted and pious Arabic merchant, Muhammad ibn 'Abdallah (pbuh)[71]. Born to the clan of Banu Hashim, of the Quraysh tribe, about 570 C.E., Muhammad, in 610 C.E, had an encounter with the angel Gabriel at Mount Hira, and was given a revelation and a message that eventually metamorphosed into the religion of Islam. Describing this landmark scenario and event, Akbar Ahmed writes:

> A mile from Makkah (Mecca) is a bleak and a forbidding mountain called Hira which rises abruptly from the earth. It has a steep and jagged face pointing towards Makkah. On top, precariously perched, is a cave. It was here that one of the most remarkable events of history took place in the seventh century. The event centered on Muhammad ibn Abdullah (son of Abdullah), who was in the habit of retreating to Hira to meditate during the month of Ramadan. In AD 610, when he was aged about forty, he heard the voice of the angel Gabriel. It ordered him to recite some of the divine verses of the Quran. The Quran was revealed; the world would henceforth know Muhammad as the Prophet of Islam.[72]

---

[69]  Ibid.

[70]  Frederick Mathewson Denny, *An Introduction to Islam*, 3rd Ed. (New Jersey: Prentice Hall, 2006), 29.

[71]  Pbuh, means peace be upon him.

[72]  Akbar S. Ahmed, *Islam Today: A Short Introduction to the Muslim World*. (New York: I.B. Tauris Publishers, 1999), 12.

This all-important event forever changed the life of Muhammad from a merchant to a religious preacher and political leader. It also brought a paradigm shift to the life of the Bedouin Arabs in the Hejaz, whose nomadic pastoral life had become urbanized with the flow of caravans in Mecca with its resultant effect of moral laxity and decadence. The event also affected the religious life of the Hejaz who practiced polytheism. Muhammad began his message as a warning on the coming judgment. He preached absolute Monotheism and the purification of the Kaaba that housed all the gods in Mecca. After much struggles and persecution, the first Umma (Muslim community) became established with those who found hope and succor in his message. Khadija, Muhammad's wife, was the first convert to Islam. Ali ibn Abu Talib, his cousin and son-in – law was the second and first male convert, followed by Abu bakar, Umar and Uthman. Bilal, a freed slave in Mecca, was first African covert to Islam, and would eventually become the first Muezzin (the one who calls for prayer) in Islam[73]

The first historical movement of Islam outside Mecca occurred in 615 C.E when some of the persecuted Muslims moved to Abyssinia in present day Ethiopia, Africa. A major historical move that would define and shape the religion of Islam occurred in 622 C.E., when Muhammad and his followers migrated from Mecca to Yathrib, which later became Medina (meaning "city of the Prophet"). This movement is called the *Hijra (migrate)*. A total of 70 people made this first *Hijra*, and these migrants are called *Al muhajirun* (the migrants). Muhammad arrived in Medina on September 24, 622.[74] This is the beginning of the Islamic Lunar calendar, and the religious and territorial expansion of Islam as a religion; an expansion and development that reached the African soil. It was in Medina that the first Mosque in Islam was built.

It was also in Medina that Prophet Muhammad (pbuh) died and was buried in 632 C.E., (A.H. 13). Today, there stands a Mosque at his burial site.

---

[73]    Denny, , *An Introduction to Islam*, 54-55.

[74]    Ibid, 55,61.

The official entrance of Islam into African soil occurred not through the direct efforts of the Prophet Muhammad, but that of his successors. As recorded by Nehemiah Levtzion and Abdin Chande,

> The task of spreading Islam beyond the Arabian Peninsula to other regions, including North Africa to the fringes of the Sahara, was left to Muhammad's successors or caliphs. Islam entered Africa within decades of its inception in the seventh century CE. In North Africa its spread was related to the empire-building process which took Islam to Morocco and Spain in the far west and to India in the east whereas in the rest of Africa its diffusion followed a different path.[75]

As early as 667 C.E., the presence of Islam was already felt in the central Sahara of Africa through various raids by Muslims. It must be recalled that raiding was part of the Arabian culture at the time of Muhammad. As recorded by Joseph Kenny, "The raids into the central Sahara by Uqba ibn-Nafi in 667, told by Ibn-Abdalhakam, opened the route to Kanem and Borno for Islam. In each town he raided, Uqba imposed a tribute of 360 slaves."[76]

Apart from raiding, the strongest factors that led to the rapid presence and expansion of Islam in much of Africa (the east coast and Horn of Africa as well as West Africa) were trade and migration. It is on record that:

> In the Sahara region and beyond it, for instance, Islam was introduced from North Africa by the Berbers, mostly members of Khārijī sects, through the trans-Saharan trade as early as the eighth or ninth century. They had their centers in the oases at the northern side of the

---

[75] Nehemiah Levtzion and Abdin Chande, "Islam: Islam in Sub-Saharan Africa" in *Encyclopedia of Religion*. Ed, Lindsay Jones, Vol. 7, 2nd ed. (Detroit: Macmillan Reference USA, 2005), 4600.

[76] Joseph Kenny, *The Spread of Islam in Nigeria: A Historical Survey.* (Enugu: Dominican Publications, 2001), 1.

Sahara in Sijilmasah, Tahart, Wargla, and Ghadames. With the expansion of this mainly salt-for-gold trade, important trading towns such as Awdaghust, Tadmeka, and Kawwar also sprang up at the southern end of the Sahara. Beyond them lay the important African states of Ghana (with Kumbi Saleh as its capital), Gao, and Kanem in the region that was known as the Sahel (which means in Arabic the "shore" of the desert). This was the region where the desert and the savanna meet and where Sahelian cities served as terminus points for a very vibrant international trade. Mālikī scholars had arrived in North Africa as early as the ninth century and had successfully won the support of both the pastoralists and traders among the Berbers who became the vehicle for dissemination of Islam into the Sahara and beyond it in West Africa.[77]

The Muslim traders needed African trading agents and associates and thus a community of African Muslims grew up along the trade routes. To facilitate this process, the African Kings were ready instruments in the hands of the Muslims traders. In the words of Kenny,

> African Kings welcomed the presence of Muslim traders in their midst for several reasons: the Muslims brought the economic advantages of long distance trade; these advantages would be greater or surer if the king himself accepted Islam, since it will give him citizenship in the Muslim *umma* with equality and brotherhood with his trading partners far away. He could then expect respect and trust from them in his dealings . . . As Islam gained ground, larger scale marketing and transport became a

---

[77] Levtzion and Chande, "Islam: Islam in Sub-Saharan Africa" 4600-4601.

> Muslim monopoly and this put pressure on traders to
> join Islam to become part of the club.[78]

An addition to trade was the military factor. Accepting Islam would also give the Kings legal immunity from attack by other Muslims. Largely because of this Military factor, Kings across the savanna, from Senegal to Lake Chad, finally declared to Islam in the 11th century. This was the result of the Murâbit (Almoravid) movement among the Sanhâja Berbers, a Sunni religious-military movement that resulted in an empire stretching from Senegal to Spain.[79]

The Muslim impact that spread across the western savanna encompassed the Mali and Songhai Empires. These Empires became the western route through which Islamic influence came to Nigeria. Kanen-Bornu Empire was the northern route of Islamic influence to Nigeria.

## 4.1.2 The origin and history of Islam in Nigeria.

The Islamic presence in Nigeria has a long history. This history, in the words of Kenny, "can conveniently be periodized by its orientation first to the Sahara and North Africa, secondly to the Atlantic, and lastly its ubiquitous orientation in the period of colonialism and independence."[80]

The Saharan connection, like in other parts West Africa, came because of trade relations. At this period, Islam had come straight across the Sahara to Borno, which was the capital of the Kanem-Bornu Empire. Borno is in the present day Borno State of Nigeria belonging to the North-East geopolitical zone. This relationship goes as far back as the 11th and 14th centuries. As described by Chima Korieh,

---

[78]  Kenny, *The Spread of Islam in Nigeria: A Historical Survey,* 1-2
[79]  Ibid, 3.
[80]  Ibid, 1.

The spread of Islam in Nigeria dates back to the eleventh century, when it first appeared in Kanem Borno in the northeast of the country. Later Islam emerged in Zaria and Kano in Hausaland through the activities of the Moslem trading community of the Dyulas, who made their way across the trade routes of the Sahara desert as the Trans-Saharan trade came to be conducted increasingly by Moslems.[81]

Although the initial contact was made in the 11th century, it was not "until the 14th and 16th centuries when Islam made a first real presence in the Northern part of Nigeria, starting from Borno."[82] As described by Kenny,

Around the late 14th century, the Kanem rulers moved to Borno in Nigeria. The *Mais* (kings of Borno) professed Islam, but only in the reign of Mai Idris Aloma (1571-1603) did the majority of the leading men of the empire become Muslims.[83]

There is a tradition that a group of Wangara Muslim clerics arrived in Katsina as well as in Kano in the middle year of the 14th century. Al-Maghili is said to have visited Katsina in 1493 and a few years later another Muslim scholar, Makhluf B. Ali, came to Katsina

---

[81]  Chima J. Korieh, "Islam and Politics in Nigeria: Historical Perspectives," in *Religion, History, and Politics in Nigeria*. Ed. Chima J. Korieh and Ugo Nwokeji. (New York: University Press of America, 2005), 112.

[82]  Joseph Omosade Awolanu, "The Encounter between African Traditional Religion and Other Religions in Nigeria" in *African Traditional Religions in Contemporary Society*, edited by Jacob K. Olupona. (New York: Paragon House, 1991), 114

[83]  Joseph Kenny, "Shariah and Christianity in Nigeria: Islam and a 'Secular' State." *Journal of Religion in Africa*, Vol. 26, Fasc. 4 (Nov., 1996), pp. 338-364.

to teach Islamic sciences. From Katsina, Islam spread to Kano and Zaria.[84] Affirming the authenticity of this tradition, Kenny writes;

> Islam in Hausaland received a strong boost from the Algerian al-Maghili (d.1504), who fled his homeland because of his strong convictions. The adoption of Islam by the Kings of Katsina and Kano seems to date from his visit in 1493. He wrote a book of advice on how to rule for King Rumfa of Kano.[85]

The Saharan and trade factor watered the ground for another phase in the spread and development of Islam in Nigeria: the period of Atlantic orientation, as Kenny called it. This period was characterized by military combats leading to the Jihad of Uthman dan Fodio in the 19th century that established the leadership and authority of the Sokoto Caliphate as the seat of power for Islam in Nigeria. What Mecca is to Islam world over, is what Sokoto is to Muslims in Nigeria. It is the home of the Sultan of Sokoto, the supreme head of Muslims in Nigeria. Describing the importance of Sokoto to Islam in Nigeria, Paden writes:

> The key to understanding Islam in Nigeria is to recognize the central place of the Sokoto Caliphate, which serves as a framework or model even today. The Sokoto caliphate, founded in the early nineteenth century by Usman Dan Fodio, continues to exert strong cultural influence in Nigeria and West Africa.[86]

Between the 14th and the 18th centuries, very few converts were made among the adherents of traditional religion. Those who confessed the Muslim faith were still practicing traditional religion,

---

[84] Peter B. Clark, *West Africa and Islam*. (London: Eduard Arnold Pub., 1982), 61

[85] Kenny, "Shariah and Christianity in Nigeria: Islam and a 'Secular' State." 338-364

[86] John N. Paden, *Faith and Politics in Nigeria*. (Washington, D.C.: U.S. Institute of Peace Press, 2008), 27.

as they were not required to make a sudden break from their native ways of worship. But a radical change came with Uthman dan Fodio. With the aim of purifying Islam from the taint of traditional religion and forming an Islamic state based on the Sharia, Fodio began his jihad, which lasted six years, in 1804. As a revivalist movement, "dan Fodio's jihad aimed at purifying Islam, to eliminate syncretism, remove all innovations contrary to the Koran, and to encourage less devout Moslems to return to orthodox Islam."[87] As recorded by Joseph Awolanu,

> Uthman dan Fodio, a Fulani born in Gobir who became an enthusiastic Muslim teacher, felt disgusted at the way his fellow Muslims were compromising with the adherents of African traditional religion. He quickly organized some of his followers into a fighting force and waged a holy war (*jihad*) against those who did not accept Islam, or those who were compromising with the traditional religion. In this way, Uthman dan Fodio forced many Hausa to boycott the traditional religion and accept Islam. He conquered the Hausaland, gained a foothold in Adamawa and Nupe areas of the North, and got entry into Ilorin, which is the gateway to the Yorubaland in the Southwest.[88]

Describing the person of Uthman dan Fodio, Levtzion and Chande write

> Shehu Usuman dan Fodio (Uthman Dan Fodio), a Fulani religious leader, belonged to the autonomous scholarly communities of Torodbe/Toronkawa who kept their distance and avoided making any accommodations with the Hausa elite of Gobir. They were neither traders nor pastoralists although they shared cultural values

---

[87] Korieh, "Islam and Politics in Nigeria: Historical Perspectives," 112.

[88] Awolanu, "The Encounter between African Traditional Religion and Other Religions in Nigeria," 115.

with the Fulani pastoralists who, like them, carried arms and excelled in horse riding.[89]

On his religious zeal and charismatic leadership, as well the remote cause of the jihad, Levtzion and Chande has this to say:

> Usuman, the charismatic and missionizing teacher, along with his followers engaged in preaching around the villages. His scrupulousness as a scholar won him many sympathizers among the oppressed and exploited peasants. He called for responsible leadership committed to a moral vision of society, not a corrupt one which ruled arbitrarily. As the tensions mounted between Usuman and the king of Gobir, Usuman, whose life was in danger, was forced to disengage from society by moving from Degel to an alternative place (Gudu) to establish a new just society based on his Islamic reformist program. In effect, he and his followers performed a *hijrah*, or migration, following the example of the prophet, a preparatory stage for the *jihad*.[90]

It is good to note that Usuman's idea of religious purity seems to have been different from the 21st Century Western understanding and thinking of religious purity. For the West, religious purity usually only involves purity of belief, while for Usuman it seems to have also included a purity of social morality that saw a purified Islam as the only means of overcoming social and economic injustice. This may explain why he attracted oppressed and exploited peasants.

On the success of this Jihad in the spread, propagation, and development of Islam in Nigeria, Levtzion and Chande state:

> Once open conflict erupted between the king of Gobir and his Muslim protagonists, Usuman declared a *jihad*, which, after its initial success, attracted other, disaffected groups, including Fulani pastoralists who

---

[89] Levtzion and Chande, "Islam: Islam in Sub-Saharan Africa" 4606.

[90] Ibid, 4606-07

resented arbitrary seizure of their stocks. These military campaigns, which lasted from 1804 to 1810, engulfed not just the Hausa states, but also western Bornu, Adamawa, Nupe, and the Yoruba state of Ilorin (the basis of Islam's later impressive inroads among the Yoruba in the forest region of Nigeria). The outcome was a sprawling empire or Sokoto caliphate, with a number of separate emirates, which was ruled by a caliph (*Amir al-Muslimin*). [91]

The effects of the Sokoto jihad were far reaching, politically, socially, culturally, and intellectually, both for Muslims and for non-Muslims in Nigeria and Africa at large. Consequently, the cultures of the areas that later came to be known as Northern Nigeria were Islamized and given a Muslim vision of history and society. The reform established in the area (Northern Nigeria and parts of the South of the Niger) new legal, administrative and educational institutions based on Muslim concepts, ideas and values. Peter Clarke and I. Linden state that, "As a result of the jihad, Islam became the spatio-temporal framework within which people thought of their history and conducted their day-to-day affairs."[92]

This second phase put into place a lasting and permanent religious structure for Islam in Nigeria. It provided machinery to further the spread of Islam into other parts of Nigeria. It also provided the basis for the third phase in the spread and development of Islam by laying the necessary foundation for Islamic influence in the period of colonialism and independence.

In the colonial period of Nigeria the propagation, spread and development of Islam was favored by several factors. As narrated by Kenny,

> The first of such factors was "the *pax Britannica*" which permitted Muslims and everyone to move freely

---

[91]   Ibid, 4607

[92]   Peter B. Clarke and I. Linden, *Islam in Modern Nigeria: A Study of a Muslim Community in a Post Independence State, 1960-1983.* (Mainz and Munich: Entwicklung und Frieden, 1984), 12.

throughout the country in pursuit of trade or livelihood. Muslims were thus able to build mosques and interact with local people throughout the country. This was not the same for Christians, who were free to move around the country, but were restricted in building churches in Muslim areas and their priests were forbidden to evangelize Muslims.[93]

Another significant factor of this period was the system of indirect rule for the north of Nigeria, that is, the former Sokoto and Borno empires. The closure of the Atlantic slave market weakened the Sokoto caliphate in the second part of the 19th century, so that it had little power to resist a British take-over. However, Instead of sweeping away these Islamic governmental systems, as the French did in their territories, the British propped them up and increased their authority. This was notable especially in areas, such as the Middle Belt, where most of the rural people were not Muslims

Furthermore, outside the Sokoto caliphate, Islam already had a foothold in Etsako and the Niger-Benue confluence area because of Nupe raiding[94], and was present in the Yoruba towns along the route to Lagos, such as Ogbomosho, Oyo, Ibadan, Sagamu, Ijebu-Ode and Abeokuta. Hausa slaves became integrated in the social and political life of these towns, and many of the chiefs declared themselves Muslims, although they continued to be actively involved in the traditional religion. In these areas Islam came to symbolize the preservation of Yoruba identity against the intrusion of British culture.

While northern Islam has been firmly reformist and separatist with regard to anything non-Islamic, Yoruba Muslims have been more accommodating. The Yoruba people are first of all Yoruba, secondly Muslim or Christian and lastly Nigerian, so that in one family you

---

93  Kenny, *The Spread of Islam in Nigeria: A Historical Survey*, 8.

94  Nupe raiding refers to the communal raiding by Muslim settlements in Nupe Kingdom. This type of raiding was typical to the Meccan tribal raiding at the time of the Prophet Muhammad.

can find both Muslims and Christians and some involvement in the traditional religion. But Yoruba Islam is more complex than it first appears. Explaining the reason for the complexity, Folaranmi Lateju writes,

> The liberated slaves returning from Brazil brought a rather progressive Islam, and their descendants have not only distinguished themselves in their personal careers, but also have led the way for development within the Muslim community. In the colonial period, they led the way in building mosques, noted for their Portuguese-Brazilian style.[95]

Discussing more the complexities of Yoruba Islam, Kenny writes,

> Yoruba Islam is not organized by the local government as it is in the north. Consequently there are innumerable societies that are the proprietors of mosques, and each has its own ideological orientation and style. There are the Lanose and Bamidele movements which reject anything western and whose men wear turbans and beards, while their women wear *ileha* (ileha is the local name of the hijab that Muslim women wear) or a black shroud covering everything, including their faces. There is the Ansar ud-deen which is also conservative, but promotes Western education. And there are branches of the Muslim Students Society and various other youth groups influenced by Saudi Wahhabi ideas calling for a reformed purist Islam.[96]

After Nigerian independence, the most prominent figure that led to the advancement and spread of Islam in Nigeria was Ahmadu

---

[95] Folaranmi Taiyewo Lateju, Mosque *Structure in Yorubaland: Their Evolution, Styles and Religious Functions,* Unpublished Ph.D. Thesis, University of Ibadan, Nigeria, 1999.

[96] Kenny, *The Spread of Islam in Nigeria: A Historical Survey,* 9.

Bello, the Sardauna of Sokoto and Premier of the Northern Region. He made numerous trips around the Arab world and was Vice-President of the newly formed, Saudi sponsored, Muslim World League (*Râbit al-'âlam al-islâmî*). This brought him a lot of Saudi money to build mosques around the north and to distribute cloth to converts in his preaching tours. In a short time, he pressurized many chiefs and prominent people to join Islam. At the same time, his preaching rallies brought many thousands into the Islamic fold.

The efforts and commitments of Bello and other Muslims from the North became instrumental to the spread of Islam beyond the northern region to the interior of the South-South geopolitical zone, as well as some parts of the South East zone.

## 4.2 The origin and history of Islam in the South-East zone.

There was a time when the South-East geopolitical zone, that is, the Igboland was seen as uncontaminated[97] by Islam. Prior to the late 1950s, there were no mosques in Igboland. But today the situation is different. Islam has made inroads into all the remote parts of the South-East. This is obvious in the increased number of mosques, Islamic educational institutions, and the growing numbers of well-educated Igbo Muslims. Describing the scenario, Simon Ottenberg wrote:

> When I first carried out field research in Afikpo community in Igbo country in 1951-1953, Anohia village seemed much like any other village there, well within the usual range of social and cultural variation. When I returned in 1959-60 the major portion of

---

[97] The term uncontaminated refers to the Igbo view that the South-East geopolitical zone is a purely Christian land. The presence of Islam would be seen as a contamination to the religious purity of the area (Igbo land).

Anohia had become Islamic, a very unusual event among the Igbo.[98]

The story of Islam in Igboland began in 1957 in Anohia, a village in Afikpo, Ebonyi State. The developments in this village illustrate well the impact the entry of Islam had on this region. Islam began to enter Anohia with the conversion of a native son, Okpani Egwani. Having been abroad for many years, he suddenly came home with his 'new religion'. Corroborating this view, Ottenberg, explained:

> In 1957 a son of Anohia, Okpani Egwani, who had been abroad for many years, suddenly returned. No one had heard from him for a long time. It is said that he was thought dead and that burial services had been performed for him. He returned a Moslem, with a small following of Moslem strangers from the north, in a number of automobiles. He had changed his name to Alhaji Ibrahim.[99]

Born in 1929 in the Ezi Ewa compound of Anohia, Egwani studied at the Afikpo Primary School, worked in Calabar and on the island of Fernando Po (now Malabor), where he learned some Spanish, and joined the Nigerian army in 1944. After his discharge he stayed at Lagos where he claims to have had a dream about God which made him travel to Egypt, Gabon and the Congo. On his voyages he joined the Muslim sect of Tijaniyya, following the spiritual leadership of Ibrahim Nyas of Kaolak, near Dakar. He joined after having a dream about this man, whom he then visited, and who converted him.[100] On his return, with a handful of Muslims he began preaching that Allah is the only true God, and encouraged people to convert to Islam. He also made use of material gifts, which he came home with to entice and win converts.

---

[98] Simon Ottenberg, "An Moslem Igbo Village." *Cahiers D'Etudes Africaines*, No. 42, Vol. 11, 1971, p.231

[99] Ibid, 238

[100] Ibid, 239.

He equally applied the use of force to win converts. Those of his converts who can be called the first Igbo Muslims were mostly those of his family and lineage members, and a few other persons. Some joined out of curiosity to learn more about this new religion, others for the sake of change, still others out of deep faith in the "new" God, Allah, and still many more out of support to their kinsman. With his homecoming, life was no longer the same for the people of Anohia. Writing on the situation, Ottenberg said:

> Egwani's return to Afikpo was a disaster for his people. He was unable to recruit most of Afikpo to the new religion. In fact the presence of Islam had negative effects on the society. First, it led to the destruction and subversion of indigenous life and culture. For example, on Sunday, October 28, 1958, in the presence of the assistant officer and a number of police, Northerners who were followers the Alhaji (Egwani) Ibrahim destroyed the shrines by taking to the secret society bush and burning it. The Anohia converts had not wished to do so themselves. The shrine pots and other items were taken from their rock resting places, their sheds, their ancestral houses, or wherever they were, and every shrine in the first ward of Anohia was burned. All but a part of the secret society bush was cut down and cleared; its shrine was also burned. The shrine in front of the men's rest house of the main ward was also destroyed, as well as the secret masks and other paraphernalia stored inside of the house.[101]

Again, the presence of Islam in Anohia engendered rancor, division and increased tension among the people. Disputes arose over the use of community property and the maintenance of traditional norms: the market, rest house, secret society bush, fishing pond, and the celebration of festivals and the non-observance of taboos. As a result, "There followed, in 1957 and 1958, a series of court

---

[101]   Ibid, 242

cases, largely instituted by the non-Moslem elders of Afikpo and non-converts from Anohia, to prevent the burning of the shrines and other contemplated changes in the village."[102] The traditional men's rest house in Anohia was forcefully turned into a mosque. This was the 'first' mosque in Igboland.

These first Igbo Muslims in Anohia did not find it easy either, as the people of Afikpo saw Islam as a threat and fought back to contain it culturally, religiously, politically, and legally. Hence, at Anohia,

> A mat fence was eventually erected to separate the two parts of the village from each other. The heart of the secret society shrine was later recovered by its priest and reestablished in the traditional section of the village. Islamic converts were barred from active participation in society, especially because of their total disregard for traditional norms. Ostracism was a potent weapon of the non—Muslims. And the fate of one Chief Iwu Egwu, a prominent leader from Ngodo village, testifies to the power of Igbo traditional society as the defender of Igbo culture and tradition. After his conversion to Islam, he was then fined by the senior Afikpo age grades[103], and was more or less ostracized by other leaders, although he was an influential man and was associated with the progressive and schooled persons in the community. After some time he withdrew from Islam and paid his five pound fine, but he never regained the stature in Afikpo he had held prior to his conversion, and was much ridiculed for his action.[104]

---

[102]   Ibid, 241

[103]   The Age grade is a traditional system of grouping together those who are born within the same period in Igboland. For example, people born within a period of 1-3 years gap are considered to be of the same age.

[104]   Ibid.

Afikpo children were taught to make fun of Muslims by shouting at them and calling them "Mallam, Mallam."[105] No doubt, the most important response of Afikpo to the Muslim threat was that of the *ekpe uke esa*, the major and most senior Afikpo age group. At the end of 1959, it called a meeting of the elders of five village groups to coordinate collective security measures against the Islamic menace, and to raise money to take the issue to court as well as to petition the Eastern Nigerian government based in Enugu. The calling together of five villages in the community is rare; it is normally carried out only when there is serious trouble between two of them or internally within a village, and only when, in either case, the matter remains unresolved. In this case, their aim was clearly to control and contain Muslim authority.[106] The *ekpe uke esa,* without asking the Muslim group to come, to present their side of the story, and to explain their religious claim, concluded that Islam should not be allowed in the land. However, at the Magistrate court in Enugu, the matter became more complex. The British colonial government that ruled the nation was pro-Islamic, while the government of the East-Central state (under whose territory both Enugu and Anioha belong), and supported the traditionalists. At the end, a consensus was reached that those natives who want to practice Islam be allowed to do so without molestations by the natives on the condition that the Muslim natives stop destroying and desecrating traditional shrines and institutions.

---

[105] The word "Mallam" is an Islamic title of respect in Nigeria. It is equivalent to the English titles "Mr" and "Sir." In Afikpo and other parts of Igboland the name Mallam was used as derogatory title to Muslims who first came into Igbo land. When I was growing up as a child in the village, every northern person in our locality who dressed in a caftan (the northern traditional garment), was seen as a Muslim, and was followed around and called Mallam or Aboki (another derogatory name for northerners, especially the Fulani cattle rearers.)

[106] Interview at Afikpo, April 4, 2009.

The first Islamic educational institution in Igboland was established in Afikpo on September 12, 1963 for the learning of Arabic and Islam, as well as for the propagation and spread of Islam in other parts of Igboland. As an affiliate of the Muslim World League, this institution is fully funded from Saudi Arabia.[107] Below are photos showing the institution in Afikpo.

Another town that played a major role in the propagation of the Islamic faith in Igboland is Nsukka. With 14 mosques, Nsukka is believed to be the most Muslim Igbo city today. Part of the reason for this is the location of Nsukka, having common boundary with Kogi, a predominant Muslim state.

Another strong center for the propagation of Islam in the South-East is Enugu.

Enugu is the home of two of the most prominent Igbo Muslims: Alhaji Abdulaziz Ude and Alhaji Yahaya Ndu. Ndu is from Ezeagu Local Government Area in Enugu State. Another, Alhaji Isah Okonkwo, is not well—known. An indigene of Akpugo in Nkanu LGA, Enugu State, he was converted into Islam as a member of the National Youth Service Corps (NYSC). He rose quickly, becoming the president of the Muslim Corpers Association in Kaduna State and the Muslim Corpers Association of Nigeria. Okonkwo was made the Chief Imam, University of Ibadan, in the 1980's.[108] One of the greatest tools for the spread of Islam in the Enugu area is the Islamic educational institution: Al Haudaa Muslim. Established in 1990 by Igbo Muslims in Enugu, and approved by the former Anambra State Government, it has a student population of about 150 students, who range in age from 3 to 12 years. Like the school in Afikpo, Al Hudaa awards scholarships to all its students, from kindergarten to elementary. About 80% of the teachers at the Islamic School in Enugu are Christian. Moreover, while they are normally allowed to practice their faith, an unusual but traditional tool of Muslim proselytism daily confronts these Christian teachers: They are paid a higher salary than public school teachers are in an

---

[107] Interview at Afikpo, April 4, 2009.

[108] Interview in Enugu, April 5, 2009.

overt and non-subtle attempt to entice them to the Islamic religion. The school authorities are, understandably, unwilling to give the source of the school's financial support; one of them could only acknowledge that the "Muslim authorities" fund it. The Chief Imam of Al Hudaa is Igbo; he was on pilgrimage to Mecca during this research. His deputy is Yoruba. One of the Igbo Imams, Alhaji Okoro, in this center became a Muslim 20 years ago.[109]

Another reason for the spread of Islam is trade. The presence of Islam in Onitsha, Owerri, Aba, Umuahia, and Arochukwu, are traceable to this factor. In the South-East geopolitical zone, Onitsha is the strongest and largest economic city, second only to Lagos in the whole of Nigeria. Its proximity to the Niger and the South-West made it a fertile ground for Muslim traders, who not only came with their merchandise but also their religion. Trade in cattle and textile brought the Muslims into Umuahia, the Abia state capital. It was from Umuahia that Islam spread to other parts of the state, including Arochukwu.[110]

Abia state proved a fertile ground for the practice of Islam, partly because of the welcoming attitude of the people, but more due to the support and encouragement of the state government that promotes religious harmony. As reported by Ben Asante,

> Every morning before the start of work, Kalu (then Abia state governor) worships in the small chapel attached to the Governor's mansion. He is joined by his lieutenants, employees and, at times, by visitors. A devout Catholic, and a demonstration of unity in a state whose population is mainly Christian, Kalu has been keen on according equal recognition for other faiths, including rebuilding a mosque in Umuahia.[111]

Various factors have been attributed to the rapid spread of Islam in Igboland. Among such factors, include Pauperization

---

[109]  Ibid.

[110]  Interview in Arochukwu, April 15, 2009.

[111]  Ben Asante, "Abia State, a model for all." *New Africa*, Dec, 2004.

before Proselytization. Adopted during the Nigeria-Biafra War (1967-1970), this policy included the post-war attempt by the Muslim-controlled Nigerian government to restrict the Igbo people only to Igbo—speaking areas of Nigeria in order to undermine and blunt their fabled business acumen; the takeover and destruction of mission schools, the engine of Igbo socio-economic, political and religious advancement; the abandoned property injustice and the ₦20.00 charade;[112] exclusion from higher position in the military, economy, and politics; the refusal to establish industries and to repair basic infrastructures—roads, water and electricity—in Igboland; and the promotion of joblessness, crime and general insecurity in the area. The intention has been to use economic pressure to make the impoverished Igbo susceptible to conversion to Islam.

Added to the above factors is undermining Christianity and Promoting Islam: This is to be achieved by making Islam the religion of success and upward mobility—by giving preference to Muslim converts in promotions in the military, civil service, contracts, and political appointments. The psychological effect has been devastating: Many Igbo executives now believe that unless the name of a Hausa-Fulani is printed on their companies' letterheads,

---

[112] During the Nigeria-Biafra civil war (1967-1970) which was overtly looked upon as a Northern-Muslim and Eastern-Christian war, the Igbos in other parts of the country came back to the east for security reasons. On going back to their various locations after the war, the Nigerian government and various state governments declared their properties as abandoned and were assigned to indigenes of those states. Again, during the war, the Biafran state that had seceded from the federal government of Nigeria began using the Biafran Pounds as their currency. After the war, the federal government of Nigeria liquidated all bank accounts belonging to the Igbos giving each person ₦20.00 in return, not minding how much he/she had in the account before or during the war. These two incidents negatively impacted the life and economy of the Igbos, who saw conversion to Islam as an easy route to repositioning oneself in the social and economic stream of the Nigerian society.

it would be impossible to win contracts in both the public and private sectors.

Female Igbo National Youth Service Corp (NYSC) members are sent to the predominantly Muslim parts of Nigeria and enticed with money, jobs, and cars in order to get them married as second or third Muslim wives.

Whatever the reason for its origin and spread, the fact is that Islam is now a permanent reality in the South-East geopolitical zone (Igboland). As recorded by Muhammad K. Muhammad in an interview with Alhaji Abdulkadir A. Obiahu, an Igbo Muslim on the occasion of his chieftaincy title as the *Defender of Igbo Muslim*:

> The Igbo people, Alhaji Abdulkadir believed, have finally decided to accept the reality of the existence of Islam because they have realized that it cannot be wished away. 'What they told me is that as Christianity will not finish in Nigeria, Islam will not finish, the best they can do is to recognize the Igbo Muslim,' Abdulkadir said.[113]

The spread of Islam through various means in Nigeria have created many suspicions in the minds of non-Muslim, at times leading to tension and conflict. Our concern is to determine what should be done, given the present reality of Islam in Nigeria and particularly in the Southeast (Igboland) zone, so that we may all live together in unity and harmony.

---

[113] Muhammad K. Muhammad, "Behold the Defender of Igbo Muslims." Daily Trust, Abuja, December 9, 2007.

# CHAPTER FIVE

# THE ORIGIN AND HISTORY OF CHRISTIANITY IN NIGERIA AND THE SOUTH-EAST ZONE.

## 5.1 The Origin and History of Christianity in Nigeria.

To understand Christianity: its origin and history in Nigeria, and in the South-East geopolitical zone, this chapter is divided into two sub-sections, beginning with a quick look at the origin and history of Christianity in general. This will help us to trace the route through which the religion entered Africa in general and Nigeria in particular down to the South-East Igboland.

5.1.1 The origin and history of Christianity: An overview.

The word 'Christianity' is a derivation of the word Christian; a term that first occurred in Act 11: 26 to refer derogatorily to followers of Jesus the Christ in Antioch. Hence, Christianity is defined and understood only in reference to the person of Christ. In fact,

> Without Christ, there would have been no gathering of
> a community that follows his way; he is the basic figure
> that holds together all those who bear his name. Without

Christ, there would have been no history of Christianity or Christians: he is basic motif, which holds and binds them into being a group. The name of Christ, which has already become a proper name in the New Testament, is thus abidingly valid, constantly obligatory and simply indispensible element in Christianity.[114]

In term of its origin, Christianity is both a revealed religion and a historical religion. As a revealed religion, "Christianity cannot be said to have had a genealogy at all. It has been classed among the "revealed" religions, and revealed religions have no genealogies; they appear for the first time when God grants the revelation to the prophets."[115] As a revealed religion, Christianity has a history that is often called "salvation history"[116] that is found in the traditional reading of the biblical account of Israel, the life of Jesus, and the rise of the early church.

Apart from being a revealed religion, Christianity also has a human history. The chronological historical origin of Christianity starts with Jesus of Nazareth, a Palestinian Jew, in the first century CE.[117] As narrated by Jaroslav Pelikan Christianity is a historical religion. It locates within the events of human history both the redemption it promises and the revelation to which it lays claim:

---

[114]  Hans Küng, *Christianity: Essence, History, and Future*. (New York: Continuum, 1998), 26

[115]  Gregory J. Riley, *The River of God: A New History of Christian Origins*. (New York: HarperCollins Publishers, 2003), 2-3

[116]  The Church's traditional interpretation of the history of salvation traces the dealings of God from Adam to Abraham, from Abraham to God's choice of the people of Israel led by Moses in Egypt. The story moves them from Moses to Joshua and the kingdom of David's Palestine, with its fall and eventual rebirth, down to the intertestamental period to Jesus and the Church's spread throughout the Roman world.

[117]  Mary Gerhart and Fabian E. Udoh, Eds. *The Christianity Reader* (Chicago: University of Chicago Press, 2007), 161.

Jesus was born under Caesar Augustus and "suffered under Pontius Pilate," at particular dates in the chronology of the history of Rome (even though the specific dates of those two events may be impossible to determine with absolute precision). It is, then, with Jesus of Nazareth that the history of Christianity takes its start. Almost everything that is known of him, however, comes from those who responded, in loyalty and obedience, to the events of his life and the content of his teaching. Therefore the history of the earliest Christian communities, to the extent that we are in a position to reconstruct it, is at the same time the history of Jesus as they remembered him.[118]

It must be noted that although the Christian history is traced back to Christ, Christ was not the explicit founder of what came to be called Christianity, or the Christian community, or the Church. He, Jesus Christ, was a Jew. Born to Mary and Joseph (his foster father),[119] he began his public ministry in 30 CE as an itinerant Jewish preacher with the call of twelve apostles, namely: Peter, Andrew, James, John, Philip, Bartholomew, Thomas, Matthew, James the son of Alpheus, Thaddaeus, Simon the Zealot, and Judas Iscariot.[120] Jesus lived and died Jewish, not Christian in 33 CE.

However, what came to be identified as Christianity or the Church emerged as a result of the interpretation of the life, teaching, message and death of Jesus by his followers. Explaining this, Hans Küng emphasizes that Christianity or

> The Church might be briefly defined as the community of those who believe in Christ. More precisely: not founded by Jesus, but emerging after his death in his name as crucified and yet living, the community of those who have become involved in the cause of Jesus

---

[118]  Jaroslav Pelikan, "Christianity: An Overview", in *Encyclopedia of Religion,* Ed, Lindsay Jones, Vol. 3, 2nd ed. (Detroit: Macmillan Reference USA, 2005), 1660.

[119]  Matthew 1:16

[120]  Matthew 10:2-3

Christ and who witness to it as hope for all men. Before Easter there was nothing more than an eschatological collective movement. A congregation, a Church, came into existence only after Easter and this too was eschatologically oriented: at first its basis was not a cult of its own, a constitution of its own, an organization of its own with definite ministries, but simply and solely the profession of faith in this Jesus as the Christ.[121]

These believers in Jesus who later became Christians did not initially see themselves as a different religious body outside Judaism. In fact, "The Christian movement began as one of the groups within Judaism,"[122] even though with time it began to see itself as the new group, the new Israel. Describing Christianity as a new movement and at the same time old, George Riley writes,

Christianity was in fact something new, but was drawn from and contained ideas very old. As a result of criticism about their recent rise on the one hand, and their own need for understanding and legitimation on the other, Christians trace their beginnings back to the Old Testament and cast themselves as the continuation of the history of Israel. Jesus and nearly all of his early followers were Jews, so their own traditions as Jews were their natural background. These Christians saw themselves as heir to the promises made to the patriarchs, Moses, David, and especially the prophets. They were the new Israel, with roots that went back through old Israel to the beginning of creation itself.[123]

Though born within Palestine and at the precinct of Judaism, Christianity arose in the historical context of the Greco-Roman

---

[121] Küng, *On Being a Christian*, (New York: Image Books, 1984) , 478.

[122] Gerhart and Udoh, *The Christianity Reader,* 161.

[123] Riley, *The River of God: A New History of Christian Origins,* 2

world; a world that deeply affected the history and development of Christianity. From this historical and geographical environment, Christianity spread to other cultures and people, including Africa.

It was during the first century CE that Christianity took root on the African continent from its sources in ancient Palestine. It spread into the regions of the late Roman Empire in North Africa and into Ethiopia and up to the Nile into Nubia.[124] Confirming the report of the early presence of Christianity in Africa, Azize Atiya writes,

> Although we lack written sources, archaeological evidence suggests an early origin for the North African churches. However, we must distinguish between two obvious centers in the first century of the preaching of Christianity on the southern shores of the Mediterranean. One center was in Cyrenaica, within reach of the influence of Alexandria. The other was in Carthage, undoubtedly influenced from neighboring Rome across the sea. Tradition associates the emergence of Christianity in Cyrenaica with the evangelization of Egypt by the apostle Mark. Participation of Libyans and people from Cyrene in the religious controversies at Jerusalem is confirmed by the Acts of the Apostles (2:10, 6:8–9). Moreover, archaeological work has revealed the existence of catacombs in Cyrene that substantiate the development of an organized church with ties to Alexandrian Christianity prior to the third century. The first mention of the church in Carthage came in the year 180, when Tertullian declared that his native Carthage was directly related to Roman apostolic authority. The church that, during the second century, produced so great a giant in the field of Christian theology as Tertullian must have had deep roots in the first century. Carthaginian Christianity was so strong and foundational that it had great influence on the

---

[124] Benjamin C. Ray, *African Religions: Symbol, Ritual, and Community,* 2nd ed. (New Jersey: Prentice Hall, 2000), 169.

theological controversies of the next several centuries within Western and Eastern Christendom.[125]

It was the Church in Carthage that produced outstanding early Church fathers and theologians like Tertullian, Cyprian and Augustine. This early presence of Christianity flourished only for about 500 years before North Africa was taken over by the Muslims. According to Benjamin Ray,

> Six centuries later [after the founding of Christianity in Africa], however, the Islamic conquest swept across North Africa and effectively abolished Christianity from the continent, except in remote parts of Egypt and Ethiopia, where small Coptic and Orthodox churches survived.[126]

Another attempt at Christianizing Africa began in the fifteenth century, this time in Sub-Saharan Africa. It is on record that,

> The Portuguese brought Christian missionaries to the western and eastern shores of Sub-Saharan Africa. A long term effort took place in the Congo under the leadership of Jesuit and later Italian Capuchin missionaries. They succeeded in converting the great king of Kongo, Alfonso I (ruled 1509-1543) and most of the nobility of the kingdom in the early decade sixteenth century.[127]

Fifty years later, in 1593, the Kingdom of Kongo collapsed, and the region fell into a cycle of devastating civil wars. Thereafter, Christianity persisted in the Kongo-speaking area and in other mission stations in the Sub-Saharan Africa on a small scale, supported by missionaries and political ties to European states. At this time,

---

[125] Azize Atiya, "Christianity: Christianity in North Africa," in *Encyclopedia of Religion*, Ed. Lindsay Jones. Vol. 3, 2nd ed. (Detroit: Macmillan Reference USA, 2005), 1677.

[126] Ray, *African Religions: Symbol, Ritual, and Community*, 169.

[127] Ibid.

the Africans, especially in Congo, perceived Christianity as a kind of initiation society and fertility cult and blended it into the local cosmology. As reported by John K. Thornton,

> Catholic priests were called *ngauga*, the same as Kongo native priests; Catholic crosses and images were called *minkisi*, the same as Kongo power objects; and the Christian God was called *Nzambi Mpungu*, the native name of the Kongo supreme god. In this period, Kongo religion as a system survived relatively intact.[128]

Stronger and enduring Christian missionary activities in West Africa came in the 18th century with the abolition of the Slave trade, and in the early 19th century, the era of colonialism in Africa. With these two phenomena, Christianity began to flourish on African soil. Reporting on the impact of the abolition of the Slave trade and the growth of Christianity in West Africa, Moses O. Ezegbe writes,

> The story of the Christian missionary advent and activities in the 18th century is linked up with the abolition of the slave trade, the emancipation of slaves, return of ex-slaves from Brazil, Portugal and the West Indies and their rehabilitation in their original homes in West Africa, particularly in Liberia, Freetown, Sierra Leone; and their settlement in Granville Town. Many of those who returned to West Africa by the end of the 18th century had already been converted to Christianity before they were brought back to West Africa . . . In their places of settlement; the Christians therefore practiced their various Christian faiths. Many of them could read and write; several were artisans, schoolmasters and evangelists.[129]

---

[128] John K. Thornton, *The Kingdom of Kongo*. (Madison: University of Wisconsin Press, 1983), 64.

[129] Moses O. Ezegbe, "The Advent of the Catholic Church in Eastern Nigeria" in *Evangelizing with gladness: A History of the*

Reporting on the impact of colonialism on the growth of Christianity in West Africa, Ray writes,

> Only when European colonialism became firmly rooted in Sub-Saharan Africa in the nineteenth century did Christian missionaries and their African catechists succeed in the making large numbers of converts. Under colonialism, the missionaries were partners with the Western political and economic force that introduced a wide range of Western values and institutions, while indoctrinating Africans with the sense of racial inferiority and a strong dislike for their own religion and culture. Under these circumstances, conversion to Christianity amounted to 'conversion' to a whole new culture: colonialism. The first African Christians, therefore, acquired a new identity. Schooled in tightly disciplined missionary compounds, they became the colonialized elite, largely divorced from their traditional culture. They made up the junior ranks of the missionary and government hierarchies and led the advances of Christianity throughout the colonies.[130]

It was from these freed slaves, especially in Freetown, Sierra Leone, and with the assistance of British colonial masters that Christianity reentered Nigeria in the 19th century after its first and failed attempt through the Portuguese in the 15th century.

## 5.1.2 The origin and history of Christianity in Nigeria.

Christianity came to Nigeria much later than Islam, which had already taken root in Northern and Southwestern Nigeria. In the words of Njoku, "Before the advent of Christian missionaries to

---

*Catholic Diocese of Umuahia (1958-2008)* Edited by M.O. Ezegbe (Umuahia: Lumen Publications, 2008), 16

[130] Ray, *African Religions: Symbol, Ritual, and Community*, 170

the territories that became Nigeria, traditional religions and Islam dominated the religious landscape."[131]

The origin of Christianity in Nigeria is traced back to the fifteenth century with the coming of the Portuguese missionaries. The first priests of the catholic diocese of Lisbon Portugal made the first attempt to plant the seed of Christianity in Nigeria during the age of exploration with their arrival in Benin in 1472.[132] This attempt covered the period between 1472—1707 in Benin City, and 1574-1708 in Warri in the Kingdom of Itsekiri.[133] It is on record that,

> The Portuguese missionaries were very active in Benin in 1485, and 1520, and on a few occasions, the Oba came close to being converted to the new religion. The missionaries were more successful in the kingdoms of Warri where two successive kings were known to have become Christians.[134]

However, the seed that was sown at this time did not bear much fruit because of the early exit of the missionaries and lack of clergy. At this time, there was not yet an ordained Nigerian Clergy. Again, the attraction and influence of traditional religion on the people contributed to the early death of Christianity at this time. It must be mentioned that Islam did not contribute to this early phase out of Christianity from Nigeria, because at this time the Christian mission ground was in the South, while the mission ground of

---

[131]  Njoku, "Economy, Politics, and the Theological Enterprise in Nigeria," 142.

[132]  Imokhai C. A., The History of the Catholic Church in Nigeria. (Onitsha: Macmillan Press, 1982), 1

[133]  Jude C. Aguwa, "Christianity and Nigeria Indigenous Culture" in Chima J Korieh and Ugo Nwekeji ed, *Religion, History, and Politics in Nigeria.* (New York: University Press of America, 2005), 14

[134]  K. C. B. Onwubiko, *A History of West Africa,* Vol. 2 (Ibadan: African Publishers Press, 1961), 196.

Islam was in the North. There was neither interaction nor conflict between the two missionary religions at this time.

A lasting Christian mission in Nigeria began in the 19th century. This time the effort was championed by the protestant churches of America and Europe at the request of Yoruba former slaves. These former slaves were converted to Christianity in America and Europe and were first settled in Sierra Leone before finally returning home to Nigeria. As recorded by Awolanu,

> Christianity was introduced into the Southern part of Nigeria as result of the liberation of slaves from the New World towards the end of the 18th century. The liberated slaves (*sic*) who returned to West Africa and to the Yorubaland preferred to continue their Christian worship . . . It was they who asked that pastors be sent to them from Freetown, Sierra Leone which was the "home" of liberated slaves in 1842.[135]

In response to this request, a team of missionaries was dispatched. In 1842, the head of the Gold Coast (now Ghana) Methodist mission, Thomas Birch Freeman opened a station in Badagry. That same year the Church Missionary Society (CMS) in Sierra Leone sent pioneer missionaries into the hinterland of Nigeria (Abeokuta).[136] Among these pioneers were Samuel Ajayi Crowther (himself a Yoruba freed slave who was later ordained in 1843), Henry Townsend, and Charles Gollmer. Capturing the whole scenario, Jude Aguwa writes,

> In 1842, the Church Missionary Society (C.M.S) arrived and established a mission in Badagry. The same year, 1842, the Methodist Church came to Abeokuta; two years later, in 1844 the C.M.S entered the same town, and then went to Lagos in 1851, Ibadan in 1853,

---

135  Awolanu, "The Encounter between African Traditional Religion and other Religions in Nigeria", 112

136  David D. Laitin, *Hegemony and Culture: Politics and Change among the Yoruba*. (Chicago: University of Chicago Press, 1986), 42

and Onitsha in 1857. The United Church of Scotland (Presbyterian Church) entered the South-South town of Calabar in 1846. The catholic mission came to Lagos in 1863 and to Onitsha in the South-East in 1885.[137]

The plans for planting Christianity in the Northern part Nigeria, which was already an Islamic territory, were also conceived in the early 19th century. The CMS and the Baptist Church championed this effort. As recorded by F. J. Kolapo,

> The Church Missionary Society's instruction to David Hinderer, who arrived Nigeria in 1849, was that he was specially set apart for the study of Hausa language, for communicating with the Hausa natives and ultimately for a missionary visit to the Hausa country. In 1850, the Southern American Baptist Mission (SABM) first set foot in Nigeria with the main goal of evangelizing among the Nupe and the Hausa. This mission was led by T. J. Bowen . . . In 1857, W. H. Clarke , another Baptist missionary, explored up to Ilorin but was disallowed by the emir from settling in the city.[138]

Between 1859 and 1877, Samuel Crowther, in the upper Niger where he set up various missions, "led an all-African missionary group to establish CMS Christian influence in the Muslim Nupe emirate. He carried out a more successful foray from the southeastern flank via the Niger River route."[139] Crowther was a tremendous success in establishing the Christian faith at Lokoja on the confluence of the Niger and Benue River in 1865. Lokoja, as a southern Nupe border town with Igala, became a perfect site to

---

[137]  Aguwa, "Christianity and Nigeria Indigenous Culture", 13
[138]  F. J. Kolapo, "making Favorable Impressions": Bishop Crowther's C.M.S. Niger Mission in Jihadist Nupe Emirate, 1859-1879" in Chima J. Korieh ed. *Religion, History, and Politics in Nigeria* ,31
[139]  Ibid, 28

launch the Christian mission into the Nupe emirate.[140] Christianity later spread to all parts of Northern Nigeria through the efforts of migrants and traders from the South, especially the South-East Igboland of Nigeria. Although suspicion and oppositions came from most Muslims, the Emirs of those Northern cities accommodated the Christian missionaries and migrants making it possible for them to build churches and schools.

Initially, the early Christians in Nigeria who were mainly freed slaves, traders and war refuges were generally isolated by the natives. It was through their efforts and perseverance that the new religion began to grow, spread and attract converts. As reported by David Laitin,

> The early Christian converts in Yorubaland (Nigeria) were mostly converted outside of their ancestral cities. In these early years, Christianity remained quarantined. In later decades, however, when Christians not only were seen to be progressive and powerful but offered literacy (hence the potential for good jobs) and free health care they won converts more broadly. Also, they offered excellent trading contacts to a growing commercial class. Christianity thus was moving from quarantine to accommodation.[141]

Apart from the role and position of the freed slaves in the introduction and spreading of Christianity in Nigeria, coupled with the dogged and tireless efforts of the missionaries, and other incentives like trade and good health, a major factor that led to the rapid spread of Christianity in Nigeria, especially in the South, was the alliance between the missionaries and the colonial masters. Each missionary moved along with the government influence of its home country. Christian mission and colonialism went hand in hand. The colonial master in most cases provided military might for the missionaries in places where they were resisted. In fact, the

---

[140] Ibid, 33.

[141] Laitin, *Hegemony and Culture*, 42-43

missionaries themselves sometimes requested such military assistance to remove obstacles to their advance.[142] Giving a concrete example of what happened in Yorubaland, Awolanu writes,

> The missionaries were backed up and given protection by the colonial administrators. For example, when Governor Cater, the British administrator in Lagos, got to know that Ijebu[143], who were very conservative in their traditional practices, were unwilling to accept Christianity, he used force to introduce "civilization" to the Ijebu and to oblige missionaries to establish schools as they had done in Lagos in order to introduce a higher standard of morality and a purer form of religion than was existing among those who were ignorant of the Bible. Eventually, in the famous Ijebu Expedition of 1892, the Ijebu were defeated, and Christianity was imposed.[144]

For 'effective' missionary activity, the missionaries (the Protestants) zoned and partitioned Nigeria, according to the missionary groups that were operating in the area: namely, the Methodists, the Anglicans (organized as the CMS), the Baptists, and the Church of Scotland Mission (Presbyterians).[145] The catholic missionaries, who saw their mission as universal and not territorial refused to be part of this partitioning. Each Christian mission and Church was hierarchically structured with headquarter either in Europe or in America. It was a mission that was characterized by much prejudice and racism, and the Nigerian way of life was described as barbaric, pagan, and heathen. The Nigerian Christians were thought of as inferior to the Europeans and Americans, and as such could not handle leadership or ministerial positions in the

---

[142] Udeani, *Inculturation as Dialogue*, 89.

[143] Ijebu is a community in Yorubaland.

[144] Awolanu, "The Encounter between African Traditional Religion and other Religions in Nigeria", 112

[145] Laitin, *Hegemony and Culture*, 44

Hyacinth Kalu

missions independently of Europeans and American missionaries. Reporting on this, Laitin writes,

> Christian church organization not only was connected with the colonialism but was also progressively racist . . . Henry Townsend, representing the first generation of European missionaries who served in the interior saw African missionaries as a threat to his career development and to the integrity of the Christian message. By the end of the nineteenth century, the next generation of European missionaries in Nigeria, imbued with a Darwinist ideology, argued that Nigerians and Africans were not yet at the stage of civilization where they could run their own church. These young men successfully demoted Bishop Samuel Crowther from his position in order to establish 'undisputed European rule' of the church.[146]

Racism,[147] among other factors, led to the establishment of Nigerian Independent and Indigenous Churches in the last quarter of the nineteenth century beginning with the Delta and Bethel Churches. Following them, Churches with African flavor began to spring up throughout Yorubaland and later in other parts of Nigeria. Describing the scenario, Laitin writes,

---

[146] Ibid, 47

[147] The White missionaries considered themselves a superior race to the blacks, as such black (Nigerian) Christians were not allowed sit to together in the same pew in the Church with the white Christians. At social gatherings, they could not eat together. Again, a black Christian, no matter how knowledgeable could not instruct or teach the white Christians who were considered superior in everything because of their racial class. This factor contributed to the blacks breaking with the missionary churches to form their own church and churches, where they were not treated as inferior people, and where they could express their religious sentiments freely without undue control by the white missionary masters.

In Southern Yorubaland, a variety of indigenous prayer groups, called *aladura* were organized. From these groups grew many churches that have attracted copious memberships. The new churches – the Cherubim and Seraphim, the Christ Apostolic Church, the Celestial Church of Christ, the Church of the Lord – offered more petitionary prayer than did the European-dominated churches, and engaged in curative medicine more in line with Yoruba/African traditional practices. But their doctrines are clearly in the Christian tradition.[148]

These Churches stress healing and fulfillment of life goals for oneself and one's family. They accept the traditional belief that sorcery and witchcraft are malevolent forces against which protection is required. Their rituals are warm and emotional in line with the African spirit of dancing and celebration. They stress personal involvement and acceptance of spirit possession and a belief in one God as other Christians do.

These indigenous churches are today grouped into three categories depending on their point of emphasis and mode of worship. These three groups are: The Healing Churches or groups that promise instant remedies, especially physical and psychological healing. The Thaumaturgical (magic groups), which are entirely syncretistic in form, borrowing from Christianity, traditional religion, occultism and from Oriental religion. Here emphasis is placed on wonder-working, magical manifestations, spirit mediumship, interpretation of dreams, protection against witchcraft, and assurance in a wide range of mundane enterprises. The Evangelical/Pentecostal groups are the third group. They combine both the so-called indigenous and foreign influences and are generally of protestant origin. Many of them are identified by their aggressive proselytism. Overall, they stress the holiness of an

---

[148]    Ibid, 48.

ethical life, the mandate to mission, baptism in the Holy Spirit, preaching and conversion.[149]

Today the umbrella uniting all Christians in Nigeria is the Christian Association of Nigeria (CAN), which has five memberships of Church affiliations:

1. The Catholic Secretariat of Nigeria (CSN)
2. The Christian Council of Nigeria (CCN)
3. The Christian Pentecostal Fellowship of Nigeria (CPFN/PFN)
4. Organization of African Instituted Churches (OAIC)
5. Evangelical Church of West Africa (ECWA) / Taraya Ekkilisiya Krist A Nigeria (TEKAN) Fellowship

## 5.2 The origin and history of Christianity in South-East zone.

Having studied the origin and history of Christianity in Nigeria in general, this part of our work will look specifically in the origin and spread of the Christianity in the South-East (Igboland) geopolitical zone.

The Church Missionary Society (CMS) sowed the first Christian seed in Igboland by establishing a mission at Onitsha on July 26, 1857. This initiative was made possible by the backing of the "awe-inspiring, influence peddling British forces and security agents, as well as the logistics of the monopolistically money bag and palm oil-holding company in Southern Nigeria, the Royal Niger Company."[150] The effort of the CMS did not bear much fruit because the Igbo people were quick to identify them with the elite group, and profiteering colonialists who were generally seen as

---

[149]  Nathaniel I. Ndiokwere, *The African Church Today and Tomorrow*, Vol. 1 (Onitsha: Effective Key Publishers, 1994), 10-20

[150]  David Asonye Ihenacho, *African Christianity Rises: A Critical Study of the Catholicism of Igbo People of Nigeria*, Vol. 1 (New York: iUniverse, Inc, 2004), 60.

unfriendly.[151] The CMS mission therefore suffered a terrible hiccup laboring under the cloud of mistrust by the indigenous people. Hence, the history of the spread of Christianity in the South-East (Igboland) is predominantly the history of Catholicism.

Twenty—Eight years after the arrival of the CMS, French Catholic missionaries, led by Fr. Joseph Lutz arrived at Onitsha in 1885. Tracing the origin of Christian missionary activities in the South-East (Igboland), Chibueze Udeani writes:

> After the initial attempt which was not able to take off for different reasons, the definite date was 27th July, 1857 when an agreement was finally executed between a missionary group of the Church Missionary Society (CMS) and Obi Akazua of Onitsha and his councilors to establish a Christian mission station at Onitsha, an Ibo (sic) town on the eastern bank of the river Niger . . . The second missionary effort towards the evangelization of Igboland came from the Roman Catholic missionaries. The first group started in 1885 under the leadership of Joseph Lutz – a French priest . . . His group like those of the CMS was well received by the King and Chiefs of Onitsha. Though the Roman Catholic missionaries started later than the CMS group, they succeeded in penetrating into the interior parts of Igboland and establishing strong footholds . . . A third missionary effort undertaken began with the Methodist society in 1892, altogether there were some six European-based missionary groups involved in the evangelization of Igboland.[152]

---

[151]  Nwosu V. A., "The Growth of the Catholic Church in Onitsha Ecclesiastical Province," in *The History of the Catholic Church in Nigeria*, 35-54,. Alexis Makozi and Afolabi Ojo, Eds. (Lagos: Macmillan, 1982)

[152]  Chibueze Udeani, *Inculturation as Dialogue: Igbo Culture and the Message of Christ*, (Amsterdam: Rodopi, 2007), 98-99.

After the cordial reception of Father Lutz and his group on December 29, 1885, they decided to settle at Onitsha as a permanent base and Headquarters for their missionary operations. It was in January 1886 that the missionaries met King Obi and his chiefs, and requested land for the establishment of a church. They explained that they had come as friends to live among them, open schools and teach their children. The King readily gave them a piece of land which, through the help of the King himself and the magnanimity of Bishop Ajayi Crowther, they later exchanged for a more elevated, commodious and spacious site formerly given to the C.M.S. through Bishop Crowther. This land is the present site of the Holy Trinity Basilica Onitsha.[153]

After the faith had been firmly planted in Onitsha and the Catholic population began to grow, the missionaries then turned their attention to places some distances away from Onitsha. Fr. Celestine Obi points out that the next places they evangelized between 1885 and 1889 were Obosi, Ossomari, Nsugbe, Umuoji, Atani, Odekpe, and Nkwelle, which they visited several times.[154] When Chief Ogbuanyinya Idigo of Aguleri heard about the missionaries and their activities in Onitsha, he invited them to visit his domain, which they did in May 1890, where they preached and made converts, who included Chief Idigo himself and some members of his household. Chief Idigo even showed them, at their own request, a place where they would build a mission house, and he helped in the establishment of a "Christian Village" in Aguleri.[155]

With the increase of converts, missionary activities and evangelism, the Vatican established the Apostolic Prefecture of the Lower Niger on April 7, 1889 with Onitsha as the headquarters,

---

[153]   Ezegbe, "The Advent of the Catholic Church in Eastern Nigeria" 21-22

[154]   Celestine A. Obi, "Background to the Planting of Catholic Christianity in the Lower Niger," in *A Hundred Years of the Catholic Church in Eastern Nigeria, (1885-1958)*. Edited by C.A. Obi (Onitsha: Africana-FEP Publishers, 1985), 24

[155]   Ibid, 43-45

and Father Joseph Emile Lutz as the first local Superior. This feat was a big bonus for the spread of the Christianity to the hinterland of the South-East and South-South (Calabar and Ikot Ekpene areas) down to Owerri and Aba between 1889 and 1912. Within this period, Fr. Lutz died in 1895. In 1905 an outstanding and vibrant missionary, Fr Joseph Shanahan became the Superior of the Lower Niger Prefecture now covering the Onitsha and the Calabar missions. Describing this expansion, Moses Ezegbe writes

> In the case of Owerri area, it has to be observed that the evangelization was undertaken by a missionary, Rev. Father John Feral of the Calabar mission. When Father Shanahan was in Calabar on a pastoral visit in early 1912 he sent Rev. Fr. Feral to go to Owerri to evangelize the town. Father Feral travelled by bicycle from Calabar to Itu, then to Ikot-Ekpene, Aba, Owerrinta and finally arrived at Owerri on March 20, 1912. He incidentally left Owerri for Ulakwo, for whatever reasons, and was eventually lured to Emekuku by the powerful chief of Emekuku then, Chief Obi Ejeshi. He finally established a mission at Emekuku in 1912 and converted many people.[156]

It was from the Owerri area that Christianity came to the Umuahia[157] area. The Umuahia area which later became a mission and eventually a diocese is the area where I come from. Narrating the spread and expansion of the Christianity to the Umuahia area, which then comprised the Umuahia and Aba zones, Celestine Obi writes:

> In Aba zone of the Umuahia area the first place to be evangelized was Umuko/Umunkpeyi, in Nvosi, which

---

[156] Ezegbe, "The Advent of the Catholic Church in Eastern Nigeria", 28

[157] The Umuahia area is now the present day Umuahia and Aba dioceses. Before the split of this area in 1990, it was administered as one (Umuahia ) diocese.

was evangelized in 1916 from Emekuku, Owerri, through Rev. Fr. Liddane, a curate under Rev. Fr. Daniel Walsh, both of whom were then at Emekuku. In the same year, Orhuru was evangelized from Calabar. In 1917, the church came to Mbutu Ngwa and C.K.C. Aba from Emekuku while Amiri was evangelized in 1918, by missionaries from C.K.C. Aba. In Umuahia zone, the first place to receive the catholic faith was Bende, in 1921, from C.K.C Aba through Rev. Fr. Herbert Whytte. Father Whytte also introduced it to Ajatta-Ibeku in 1922; and Rev. Fr. Daniel Walsh brought it to Nsirimo in the same year from Emekuku. In 1923, three other centers were established. These are St. Peters Ikwuano, through Calabar, St. Michael's Umuahia town and St. Charles Old Umuahia, through Ajatta Ibeku.[158]

The Umuahia area was eventually elevated to a diocese for grassroots evangelization in 1958 with Bishop Anthony Gogo Nwedo[159] of blessed memory as the first bishop. Upon his retirement in 1990, Bishop Lucius Ugorji became the incumbent bishop. The Aba zone was created a diocese in 1990 with Bishop Valentine Ezeonyia, as the first and incumbent bishop.

Generally, the missionaries that came to the South-East (Igboland) saw something positive among the people that became a vehicle to spread their message. That is, the Igbo language. According to Christopher Ejizu,

> In spite of their disdain for the indigenous religious culture, pioneer Christian missionaries in general (whether Roman Catholic or Protestant), knew pretty well they had to depend on the indigenous language to communicate the gospel message to the people. While

---

[158] Obi, "Background to the Planting of Catholic Christianity in the Lower Niger," 222.

[159] Bishop Nwedo is the one who ordained me to the Catholic priesthood in 1995.

the doctrines and principal religious ideas remained those of their respective Christian traditions, the local language as the primary medium of communication with their host, provided the bulk of the concepts, terms and linguistic symbols and imageries. That is not all. It set limit to thought and understanding of the received message of the missionaries.[160]

Another area worth mentioning is that the missionary activities brought to an end the *OSU*[161] caste system that was practiced in some part of Igbo land. It is also a common knowledge that missionaries abolished the killing of twins[162] in Igboland.

The missionaries also affected Igboland positively in the area of education, although the education they brought was a means of winning converts from the traditional religion. Most important was the introduction of western medicine to Igbo land by the missionaries. According to Awolalu,

> In addition to Western education, medicine and technology also came through the missionaries. These improved people's health, reduced infant mortality, put under control diseases and ailments, which people dreaded – for example, small pox, malaria, stomach pain, and the like – discouraged superstition and fear and brought about better conditions of living.[163]

---

[160] Christopher Ejizu, *The Influence of African Indigeneous Religions on Roman Catholicsm, The Igbo Example.* http://www.afrikaworld.net/afrel/ejizu-atrcath.htm (accessed May 22, 2008)

[161] An Osu is someone dedicated to the gods as a sacrificial offering.

[162] Before the coming of Christianity to Igboland, the birth of twins was considered a taboo and the babies were killed. The Christian missionaries began first by rescuing such twin babies, and later succeeded in abolishing the killing of twins.

[163] Awolanu, "The Encounter between African Traditional Religion and other Religions in Nigeria", 114

After the Independence of Nigeria in 1960, there was a renewed zeal of Christian activities in the South-East (Igboland), especially on the part of the Protestants. This new zeal has been attributed to migrations and movements from one part of the country to another. Today in Igboland every Christian denomination (Orthodox, Catholic, Protestants, Indigenous Churches, Evangelicals and Pentecostals) are found in communities of the South-East.

In all, Christianity in Africa, Nigeria and Igbo land has undergone various processes of change, adaptation and inculturation. For instance, the missionaries who brought Christianity to us, together with their African helpers, were devout, sincere and dedicated men and women. But they were not theologians; some of them had little education, and most of the native evangelists and catechists were either illiterate or had only formal learning. These workers were primarily more concerned with practical evangelism, education and medical care, than with any theological and or pastoral issues arising from the presence of Christianity in its relation with the host communities who were predominantly followers of ATR. Mission Christianity was not from the start prepared to enter into dialogue or encounter with the traditional religion, which was regarded as idolatry. However, with attainment of independence by most African nations, including Nigeria, a new awareness and interest in African religion and philosophy began to re-emerge, leading to a reassessment of the relationship between Christianity and ATR. This awareness gave birth to the theology of inculturation, and the various movements and efforts towards adapting the Christian religion to become truly African. Perhaps the most important, though not unique, phenomenon of this movement of inculturation and adaptation is the rise and growth of many Independent and Indigenous Churches in Nigeria and Africa as a whole, whose major approach is the indigenization, interpretation, and application of Christianity in a way that is more practical and meaningful to Africans, by mixing Christian rites and ATR rituals together or by giving Christian rituals an African name and expression. With this trend, the main stream Christian churches have today begun to discuss and find ways, both in theory and practice, to relate better to traditional religion and culture, and to become more relevant in the lives of the Nigerian-African people.

# CONCLUSION

There is a new awareness on the role and place of religion in the Nigerian society today. It is becoming clearer to many followers of religion that their own religion does not have all the answers to the entire problem facing the nation. There has become an increasing effort towards learning from each other and collaborating with each other in the interest of peace, national unity, and human development.

Looking at the growth and strength of the three religions in Nigeria, one would see that ATR is fast disappearing in the public life of most Nigerians; it does not have the firm grip it used to have on society about a millennium ago. On the other hand, Islam and Christianity, which hitherto were considered foreign religions, have today become indigenized. To some extent, they have become more traditional than the African Traditional Religion to most Nigerians. Overall, these three religions are positively impacting peoples live and transforming society, though areas of conflicts still abound among them.

One thing that should be borne in mind by every Nigerian, religious affiliation notwithstanding, is that though tribe and tongue may differ, our religions and geo-political zones as well as political affiliations may differ, we are all sisters and brothers, and should treat each other as such. Perhaps, the best way to illustrate this fact of our fellowship and oneness is by relating this ancient Middle East story. An ancient Middle Eastern story tells of a traveler in a desert, who, at a certain point, notices at a distance a horrible and violent monster making its way towards him. Obviously, the traveler is frightened. As the monster gets closer, the traveler being able to see him clearer, notices that it is not a monster but a man: an ugly man, but a man nonetheless. After awhile, the traveler begins to notice him better and realizes in the end, that the man is not that ugly at all. Finally, when he looks into his eyes, he recognizes that he is his brother.

In our day, many Christians, Muslims, and ATR happen to meet each other as in the desert night, where the human appearance is completely distorted. Muslims look at Christians as enemies and rivals, they look at ATR as infidels and polytheists as described in their holy books. Christians, on the other hand, see in Muslims the threatening monster of religious intolerance that killed their brothers and sisters. The insidious desert in which we walk and the deceiving night, which has fallen indiscriminately upon all, Christians and Muslims, and ATR in Nigeria, are not new phenomena. One thing is clear, our sad memories of violence can still be overcome for a brighter tomorrow. With interfaith relationships, we will rediscover the long brotherhood we share as one Nigeria.

# BIBLIOGRAPHY

1. Achebe, Chinua. *Things Fall Apart.* New York: Anchor Books, 1994.

2. Adogame, Afe. "Politicization of Religion and Religionization of Politics in Nigeria", in *Religion, History, and Politics in Nigeria: Essays in Honor of Ogbu U. Kalu.* Edited by Chima J. Korieh & Ugo G. Nwokeji. New York: University of America Press, 2005.

3. Aguwa, Jude C. "Christianity and Nigeria Indigenous Culture" in Chima J Korieh and Ugo Nwekeji ed, *Religion, History, and Politics in Nigeria: Essays in Honor of Ogbu U. Kalu.* New York: University Press of America, 2005.

4. Ahmed, Akbar S. *Islam Today: A Short Introduction to the Muslim World.* New York: I.B. Tauris Publishers, 1999.

5. Arinze, Francis. *Pastoral Attention to African Traditional Religion.* http://www.afrikaworld.net/afrel/vatican.html

6. Asante, Ben. "Abia State, a model for all." *New Africa.* Dec, 2004.

7. Atiya, Azize. "Christianity: Christianity in North Africa," in *Encyclopedia of Religion,* Ed. Lindsay Jones. Vol. 3, 2nd ed. Detroit: Macmillan Reference USA, 2005.

8. Awolalu, Joseph Omosade. "The Encounter between African Traditional Religion and Other Religions

in Nigeria" in *African Traditional Religions in Contemporary Society,* edited by Jacob K. Olupona. New York: Paragon House, 1991.

9. Barrett, David, ed. *The World Christian Encyclopedia.* Nairobi: Oxford Press, 1982.

10. Clarke, Peter B. *West Africa and Islam.* London: Eduard Arnold Pub., 1982.

11. Clarke, Peter B. & I. Linden. *Islam in Modern Nigeria: A Study of a Muslim Community in a Post Independence State, 1960-1983.* Mainz and Munich: Entwicklung und Frieden, 1984.

12. Denny, Frederick Mathewson. *An Introduction to Islam,* 3rd Ed. New Jersey: Prentice Hall, 2006.

13. Ejizu, Christopher. "The Influence of African Indigenous Religions on Roman Catholicism, the Igbo Example", in *African Theological Journal* 17, 1988.

14. Ezegbe, Moses O. "The Advent of the Catholic Church in Eastern Nigeria" in *Evangelizing with gladness: A History of the Catholic Diocese of Umuahia (1958-2008)* Edited by M. O. Ezegbe. Umuahia: Lumen Publications, 2008.

15. Falola, Toyin. *Violence in Nigeria: The Crisis of Religious Politics and Secular Ideologies.* New York: University of Rochester press, 1998.

16. Falola, Toyin & Matthew Heaton. *A History of Nigeria.* New York: Cambridge University Press, 2007.

17. Garvie, Alfred E. *The Christian Belief in God in Relation to Religion and Philosophy.* London: Hodder and Stoughton, 1933.

18. Gerhart, Mary & Fabian E. Udoh, Eds. *The Christianity Reader.* Chicago: University of Chicago Press, 2007.

19. Haneef, Suzanne. *Islam: The Path of God.* Chicago: Kazi Publications, Inc., 1996.

20. Hopfe, Lewis M. & Mark R. Woodward. *Religions of the World, 8th Ed.* New Jersey: Prentice Hall, 2001.

21. Idowu, Bolaji E. *African Traditional Religion: A Definition.* New York: Orbis Books, 1975.

22. Ihenacho, David Asonye. *African Christianity Rises: A Critical Study of the Catholicism of the Igbo People of Nigeria, Vol. I.* New York: iUniverse, Inc., 2004.

23. Ilesanmi, Simeon O. *Religious Plurality and the Nigerian State.* Ohio: Center for International Studies, 1997.

24. Imo, Cyril O. *Religion and the Unity of the Nigerian Nation.* Uppsala: Almqvist & Wiksell International, 1995.

25. Imokhai C. A. *The History of the Catholic Church in Nigeria. Onitsha*: Macmillan Press, 1982.

26. Kenny, Joseph. *The Spread of Islam in Nigeria: A Historical Survey.* Enugu: Dominican Publications, 2001.

27. Kenny, Joseph. "Shariah and Christianity in Nigeria: Islam and a 'Secular' State." *Journal of Religion in Africa.* Vol. 26, Fasc. 4, Nov., 1996.

28. Kolapo, F. J. "Making Favorable Impressions": Bishop Crowther's C.M.S. Niger Mission in Jihadist Nupe Emirate, 1859-1879" in Chima J. Korieh ed. *Religion, History, and Politics in Nigeria.* New York: University Press of America, 2005.

29. Korieh, Chima J. "Islam and Politics in Nigeria: Historical Perspectives," in *Religion, History, and Politics in Nigeria Essays in Honor of Ogbu U. Kalu,* Ed. Chima J. Korieh and Ugo Nwokeji. New York: University Press of America, 2005.

30. Korieh, Chima J. & Ugo G. Nwokeji. *Religion, History, and Politics in Nigeria: Essays in Honor of Ogbu U. Kalu.* New York: University Press of America, Inc., 2005.

31. Kukah, Matthew Hassan. *Democracy and Civil Society in Nigeria*. Ibadan: Spectrum Books, 2003.

32. Küng, Hans. *Christianity: Essence, History, and Future*. New York: Continuum, 1998.

33. Laitin, David D. *Hegemony and Culture: Politics and Change among the Yoruba*. Chicago: University of Chicago Press, 1986.

34. Lateju, Folaranmi Taiyewo. *Mosque Structure in Yorubaland: Their Evolution, Styles and Religious Functions*. Unpublished Ph.D. Thesis, University of Ibadan, Nigeria, 1999.

35. Lefebure, Leo D. *Revelation, the Religions, and Violence*. New York: Orbis Books, 2000.

36. Levtzion, Nehemiah & Abdin Chande. "Islam: Islam in Sub-Saharan Africa" in *Encyclopedia of Religion*. Ed, Lindsay Jones, Vol. 7, 2nd ed. Detroit: Macmillan Reference USA, 2005.

37. Mbiti, John S. *African Religions and Philosophy, 2nd ed*. London: Heinemann, 1989.

38. Mbiti, John S. *Introduction to African Religion, 2nd ed*. Ibadan: Heinemann, 1991.

39. Muhammad, Muhammad K. "Behold the Defender of Igbo Muslims." *Daily Trust* Abuja, December 9, 2007.

40. Ndiokwere, Nathaniel I. *The African Church, Today and Tomorrow, vol. I*. Onitsha: Effective Key Publisher, 1994.

41. Nigeria: Central Intelligence Agency. The World FactBook. https://www.cia.gov/library/publications/the-world-factbook/geos/ni.html

42. "Nigerians meld Christianity, Islam with ancient practices" in *World Wide Religious News*. October 14, 2007. http://www.wwrn.org/article.php?idd=26568&sec=con=60

43. Njoku, Anthony Chukwudi. "Economy, Politics, and the Theological Enterprise in Nigeria," in

*Religion, History, and Politics in Nigeria: Essays in Honor of Ogbu U. Kalu.* Chima J. Korie & G. Ugo Nwokeji (eds). New York: University Press of America, 2005.

44. Nwosu, V. A., "The Growth of the Catholic Church in Onitsha Ecclesiastical Province," in *The History of the Catholic Church in Nigeria.* Alexis Makozi and Afolabi Ojo, Eds. Lagos: Macmillan, 1982.

45. Obi, Celestine A. "Background to the Planting of Catholic Christianity in the Lower Niger," in *A Hundred Years of the Catholic Church in Eastern Nigeria, (1885-1958).* Edited by C. A. Obi. Onitsha: Africana-FEP Publishers, 1985.

46. Olupona, Jacob K. ed. *African Traditional Religion in Contemporary Society.* New York: Paragon House, 1999.

47. Onwubiko, K. C. B. *A History of West Africa, Vol. 2.* Ibadan: African Publishers Press, 1961.

48. Oranika, Paul. *Nigeria: One Nation, Two Systems.* Baltimore: Publish America, 2004.

49. Ottenberg, Simon. "An Moslem Igbo Village." *Cahiers D'Etudes Africaines*, No. 42, Vol. 11, 1971.

50. Paden, John N. *Faith and Politics in Nigeria.* Washington, D.C.: U.S. Institute of Peace, 2008.

51. Pelikan, Jaroslav. "Christianity: An Overview", in *Encyclopedia of Religion*, Ed, Lindsay Jones, Vol. 3, 2nd ed. Detroit: Macmillan Reference USA, 2005.

52. Rahman, Fazlur. "Islam: An Overview" in *Encyclopedia of Religion.* Ed, Lindsay Jones, Vol. 7, 2nd ed. Detroit: Macmillan Reference USA, 2005.

53. Ray, Benjamin C. *African Religions: Symbol, Ritual, and Community, 2nd ed.* New Jersey: Prentice Hall, 2000.

54. Riley, Gregory J. *The River of God: A New History of Christian Origins.* New York: HarperCollins Publishers, 2003.

55. Ritchie, Ian. *African Theology and Social Change: An Anthropological Approach.* Toronto: Wycliffe College, 1999.

56. The 1999 Constitution of the Federal Republic of Nigeria.

57. The Islamic Affairs Department of the Embassy of Saudi Arabia. *Understanding Islam and the Muslims.* Washington DC, 1989.

58. Thornton, John K. *The Kingdom of Kongo.* Madison: University of Wisconsin Press, 1983.

59. Udeani, Chibueze. *Inculturation as Dialogue: Igbo Culture and the Message of Christ.* Amsterdam: Rodopi, 2007.

60. Water, Mark. *Encyclopedia of World Religions, Cults and the Occult.* London: John Hunt Publishing Ltd, 2006.

61. Wellman, James K. Jr. "Religion and Violence: Past, Present, and Future," in *James K. Wellman's ed., Belief and Bloodshed: Religion and Violence across Time and Tradition.* New York: Rowman & Littlefield Publishers, Inc., 2007